A
PLANTSMAN'S GUIDE TO
CHRYSANTHEMUMS
JACK WOOLMAN

A PLANTSMAN'S GUIDE TO
CHRYSANTHEMUMS

JACK WOOLMAN

SERIES EDITOR
ALAN TOOGOOD

WARD LOCK

First published in Great Britain in 1989
by Ward Lock Limited, 8 Clifford Street
London W1X 1RB

House editor Denis Ingram

Text filmset in Times Roman
by Dorchester Typesetting

Printed and bound in Great Britain by
BPCC Hazell Books Ltd
Member of BPCC Ltd
Aylesbury, Bucks, England

British Library Cataloguing in Publication Data

Woolman, Jack
  A plantsman's guide to chrysanthemums.
  1. Gardens.   Chrysanthemums.   Cultivation
  I. Title   II. Series
  635.9'3355

ISBN 0-7063-6741-3

CONTENTS

Editor's Foreword □ 11

CHAPTER ONE
Past and Present □ 13

CHAPTER TWO
Planting Ideas □ 21

CHAPTER THREE
Choosing the Best □ 37

CHAPTER FOUR
General Cultivation □ 79

CHAPTER FIVE
Propagation □ 107

Appendix □ 117
Index □ 122

PUBLISHER'S NOTE

Readers are requested to note that in order to make the text intelligible in both hemispheres, plant flowering times, etc. are described in terms of seasons, not months. The following table provides an approximate 'translation' of seasons into months for the two hemispheres.

Northern Hemisphere		Southern Hemisphere
Mid-winter	= January	= Mid-summer
Late winter	= February	= Late summer
Early spring	= March	= Early autumn
Mid-spring	= April	= Mid-autumn
Late spring	= May	= Late autumn
Early summer	= June	= Early winter
Mid-summer	= July	= Mid-winter
Late summer	= August	= Late winter
Early autumn	= September	= Early spring
Mid-autumn	= October	= Mid-spring
Late autumn	= November	= Late spring
Early winter	= December	= Early summer

Captions for colour photographs on chapter-opening pages:

Pp. 12-13 'Bronze Fairie'. An attractive colour sport from the garden pompon Fairie. Excellent as a border or bedding plant.
Pp. 20-21 The hardy Spartan chrysanthemums used as a bedding plant in association with annuals.
Pp. 36-37 'Fairweather'. A neat late flowering incurved. Useful for cut flower or exhibition.
Pp. 78-79 'Cameo'. Another of the weather resistant garden pompon varieties well worth growing.
Pp. 106-107 'Denise'. The pompon varieties are excellent for garden bedding and are very weather resistant.
Pp. 116-117 'Fairie'. A lovely garden variety which needs little attention and has a long flowering period.

EDITOR'S FOREWORD

This unique series takes a completely fresh look at the most popular garden and greenhouse plants.

Written by a team of leading specialists, yet suitable for novice and more experienced gardener alike, the series considers modern uses of the plants, including refreshing ideas for combining them with other garden or greenhouse plants. This should appeal to the more general gardener who, unlike the specialist, does not want to devote a large part of the garden to a particular plant. Many of the planting schemes and modern uses are beautifully illustrated in colour.

The extensive A–Z lists describe in great detail hundreds of the best varieties and species available today.

For the historically-minded, each book opens with a brief history of the subject up to the present day and, as

appropriate, looks at the developments by plant breeders.

The books cover all you need to know about growing and propagating. The former embraces such aspects as suitable sites and soils, planting methods, all-year-round care and how to combat pests, diseases and disorders.

Propagation includes raising plants from seeds and by vegetative means, as appropriate.

For each subject there is a society (sometimes more), full details of which round-off each book.

The plants that make up this series are very popular and examples can be found in many gardens. However, it is hoped that these books will encourage gardeners to try some of the better, or perhaps more unusual, varieties; ensure some stunning plant associations; and result in the plants being grown well.

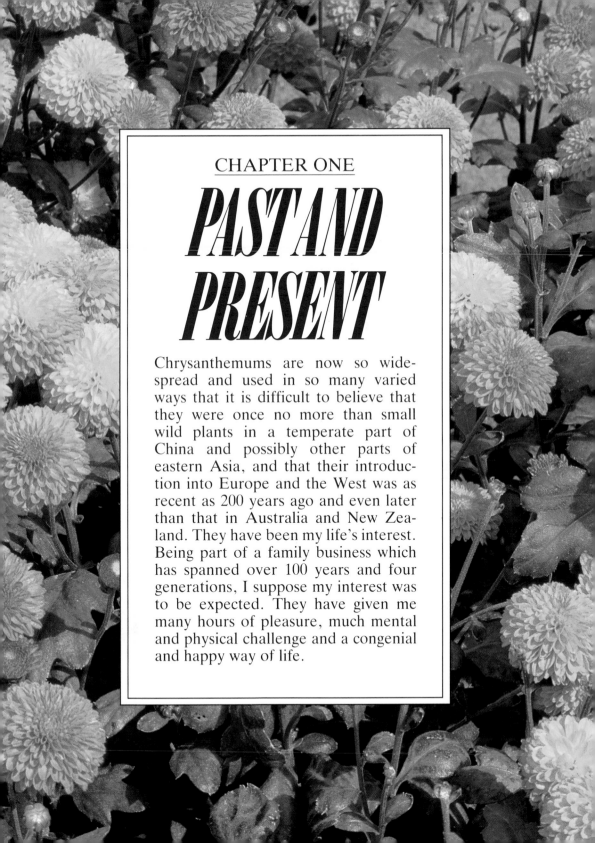

CHAPTER ONE

PAST AND PRESENT

Chrysanthemums are now so widespread and used in so many varied ways that it is difficult to believe that they were once no more than small wild plants in a temperate part of China and possibly other parts of eastern Asia, and that their introduction into Europe and the West was as recent as 200 years ago and even later than that in Australia and New Zealand. They have been my life's interest. Being part of a family business which has spanned over 100 years and four generations, I suppose my interest was to be expected. They have given me many hours of pleasure, much mental and physical challenge and a congenial and happy way of life.

What are chrysanthemums, from whence did they reach us and what can they do for the amateur gardener's satisfaction? The types we see nowadays at the flower shows and in gardens are very different from the original wild species. Chrysanthemum is really quite an apt name, coming from the Greek *chrysos*, gold and *anthos*, flower, 'the golden flower': we still love the beautiful yellow ones which are so cheerful on a dull day in autumn or winter.

EARLY REFERENCES

Although the name is Greek, the wild species originated in China; in one of the Confucian classics, *The Book of Rites*, written some 2500 years ago, there is a reference to, 'The late autumn moon and the yellow flowers of the chrysanthemum'. In those times long past they were sought not only for their beauty but also for their edible and medicinal attributes – one old Chinese book declaring, 'In Lixian county in the Nanyang area lies a pool encircled with chrysanthemums and those who partake of its waters live to a long life'. Due to this belief it became a popular custom to plant chrysanthemums around ponds and wells and thus obtain this benefit.

Another book of the time tells its readers that the chrysanthemum shoots can be eaten as a vegetable, used as a medicine, as an ingredient in making wine *and* for stuffing pillows, making it indispensable to a gentleman in rustic seclusion! Other scholars have written that 'it is chaste and steadfast by nature and blooms late when frost causes other plants to die'. That remains one of its virtues.

If you go to China you may be able to taste connoisseur dishes using the chrysanthemum. For example, from the book *Chinese Chrysanthemums*, compiled by Beijing Bureau of Parks and Gardens and Beijing Chrysanthemum Society, we have Chrysanthemum Pork, for which it says 'take slices of tender pork impregnated with syrup and garnished with chrysanthemum petals which introduce a subtle aroma'! Such gourmet delights as chrysanthemum and fish porridge, fried chrysanthemum leaves, chrysanthemum wine and tea or chrysanthemum hotpot (instant boiled slices of mutton with chrysanthemum petals) would, I am sure, be a memorable experience.

During the 8th to 10th centuries, chrysanthemums were introduced to Japan via Korea. The Japanese, using both Chinese and their own wild species, made tremendous developments with them. Their popularity and importance became such that a stylized form of a single chrysanthemum bloom was adopted as the crest and official seal of the Emperor and the Imperial Order of the Chrysanthemum became the highest order in the land.

INTRODUCTION INTO EUROPE

Plants introduced into Holland in the 17th century were subsequently lost, so the real beginning of chrysanthemums in Europe was in 1789 when a Captain Blanchard returned from a trading trip in the Far East with three varieties; two died but one, subsequently known as 'Old Purple', survived. It became increasingly popular in France and eventually reached Kew Gardens in England. Gradually others were added and by 1826 there were around 50 different named varieties in Britain.

In 1843 the Royal Horticultural Society sent Robert Fortune to China and he brought back what became known as the 'Chusan Daisy'. This was the forerunner of the present pompon-type chrysanthemum. In 1860 he was sent to Japan on another plant hunting trip that proved to be of even greater significance, bringing back some very different varieties from which the present range of types and colours has developed. The earlier Chinese chrysanthemums were mostly of a tight incurved form and with a limited colour range whereas those from Japan were extremely varied in both form and colour. Consequently, for many years the incurved varieties were known as Chinese and the large reflexed and curly types as Japanese chrysanthemums. These titles are sometimes used even now.

Both interest and cultivation increased and in France in 1826 a retired infantry officer of the French army, and a veteran of the Napoleonic campaigns, produced the first European seedlings and he was soon followed by a number of other enthusiasts. The first record of successful cross breeding in England was in 1832 when Isaac Wheeler was awarded a silver medal by the Horticultural Society for producing chrysanthemum seedlings.

In 1829 the first show by a local society was held at Norwich and this was followed by the formation of chrysanthemum societies at Birmingham and Swansea.

Back in Versailles, France, in 1838, John Salter established a nursery where he carried out development of the flower which proved to be of great importance. Due to political disturbances he moved to England in 1848 and continued to provide many new and improved varieties until he retired in 1869.

It is worth noting that in 1846 a society was formed which was called The Stoke Newington Florists' Society for the Cultivation and Exhibition of Chrysanthemums. Subsequently – perhaps the title was a little heavy! – it became the Borough of Hackney Society and eventually the still flourishing National Chrysanthemum Society of Britain.

THE FIRST EARLY-FLOWERING VARIETIES

It was not until after this date that early flowering chrysanthemums became available, and even then there were only a few button pompon varieties and they did not flower until mid-autumn. Although these became quite popular, the main interest remained with the exhibition types, which bloomed in late autumn and early winter.

There was not much literature on the cultivation of chrysanthemums available

at that time, additional knowledge having to be picked up from lectures and demonstrations at the numerous societies which were starting throughout the country. It is on record, however, that Mr Dale and Samuel Broome from London's Inner Temple, where regular shows were held, and Mr Shirley Hibberd, also of London, produced a treatise around 1850–60, following which great strides were made. New varieties were introduced from France and the Channel Islands and the benefit of Mr Fortune's Japanese visit became increasingly apparent.

INTRODUCTION INTO U.S.A. AND AUSTRALIA

Towards the end of the 19th century chrysanthemums were introduced into the United States of America and rapidly became popular. In due course enthusiasts began breeding them and a great rivalry developed between raisers in Britain, the Continent and North America. The early-flowering garden varieties seem to have gained considerable benefit from this.

At about this time Thos. W. Pockett was growing and breeding chrysanthemums in Victoria, Australia, with many of his successful varieties being sent to Europe and the United States of America. By now, the chrysanthemum was becoming the worldwide favourite we know today. Further development took

'Madame Jeanne Chaure'. This illustrates the loose formation of the decorative varieties of the time (1896).

place between 1918 and 1939 and interest in the flower continued to flourish.

Up to this time, however, development had been in new varieties of similar characteristics and treatment to those which had been available for many years. After World War II ended in 1945, there was a basic change.

AFTER WORLD WAR II

Although the exhibition types continued even as before, fresh techniques now allowed late-flowering varieties to be crossed successfully with the earlier garden flowering types, thereby greatly increasing the variety available in the latter. (It is interesting to note, however, that in improving the size and colour range of the garden varieties, their hardiness and weather resistance were weakened and these qualities had to be regained later by further breeding and selection.)

At the same time the florist flower section also changed completely as a result of new scientific discoveries, and a quite separate approach in growing techniques was developed. Before 1939 the commercial chrysanthemum grower used the same system as the amateur exhibitor, simply growing on a larger scale. Early garden varieties were grown in the open ground and flowered from late summer until mid-autumn; mid-season (late autumn) and late (winter) flowering varieties were grown in pots in the open during the summer and brought into greenhouses to flower. After 1946 the now enormous 'All the

Year Round' (AYR) industry began to take off, wherein there are no earlies, mid-season and lates, plants being grown in beds under glass throughout the year, given extra light for a period of growth and then extra dark by blacking out to produce buds and flowers. Varieties are divided into 10-week, 12-week and other groups, according to their response to this treatment, and one batch follows another throughout the year.

It is interesting to consider the background to this change. For some time before the Second World War research was taking place to discover just what brought chrysanthemums into flower. I remember in the late 1930s Professor Schwabe, who was working on this problem, coming to the nursery in Shirley and arranging for my father, John Woolman, V.M.H., to carry out larger-scale experiments than could be done under his laboratory conditions. Gradually photoperiodism, as it was called, was discovered, describing how the hours of light in each day controlled the type of growth of the plant. Less than about 14 hours light – short days – produced flower buds; while more than 14 hours light – long days – vegetative growth. Later it was realized that temperatures and the maturity of the plant were also involved, but basically at a temperature of approximately 15°C (60°F) a plant will make flower buds in short days and grow vegetatively in long days.

The early flowering garden varieties are more temperature and less day-length responsive. The whole of the vast AYR chrysanthemum industry is now based on this, because of course, it enables growers to produce blooms at exactly the time they wish.

Soon after this time there was a change in the breeding of chrysanthemums, with one group concentrating on developing the AYR commercial varieties, where the characters needed were different from the traditional requirements, and another group, including nurserymen and amateurs, continuing with the types required by the amateur gardener and exhibitor. In fact in recent years there has been an upsurge of interest among the latter and more new varieties are being developed by the amateur growers than we have seen for many years. This can only be good news for the ordinary gardener.

From the 1950s early garden chrysanthemums were continuing to improve noticeably both in colour and size. Breeders such as Riley's of Woolley Moor, Derbyshire, were instrumental in this and varieties such as 'Sylvia Riley' were widely grown for many years. They are still specializing in the early varieties, particularly the traditional disbud blooms and more recently spray types sent out under the Pennine label. They have, over the years played a major part in the development of the modern early chrysanthemum.

A major contribution of a different kind, the garden pompons, came from J. & T. Johnson of Tibshelf, also in Derbyshire, and many of their varieties such as 'Cameo' are still widely grown today.

In 1955 there arrived two early

flowering varieties, 'Ermine' and 'Evelyn Bush', which for their time were quite outstanding and dominated both exhibition and cut flower sections for many years. They were the offerings of Harry Shoesmith, V.M.H., from Woking, whose firm also contributed many of the best greenhouse-flowering varieties, including 'May Shoesmith' (1949) and 'Balcombe Perfection' (1950).

Among the leading breeders of greenhouse-flowering varieties was my father, John Woolman, V.M.H. In earlier years he specialized in Large Exhibition varieties, introducing 'Green Goddess' (1956) which rapidly became a best seller, 'Jessie Habgood' (1948), 'Phil Houghton' (1973) and many others which were and still are winners of top awards. He also bred many excellent greenhouse-flowering incurved and decorative varieties, from which I should mention 'Vera Woolman' (1953) and 'Shirley Model' (1964), which were both outstanding in their time. Among his successes in the early-flowering section was 'John Woolman' (1952), which dominated its section in the exhibition world for years and was also widely grown for the cut flower market. Since his death in 1973, I have continued to breed new chrysanthemums based on his earlier work. Over the years the early flowerers have assimilated the best qualities of the greenhouse varieties, until now they are at least their equals.

The latest development in both early- and late-flowering chrysanthemums is the production of the modern sprays for exhibition and cut flowers, or garden display. These have made quite remarkable advances under the skill of a number of able breeders, including Philip Rowe of the Somerset firm, Frank Rowe, and they are the success story of recent years. Previously sprays were just ordinary varieties grown without disbudding, some being more suitable than others. Nowadays you can grow a spray which is almost a bouquet in itself of beautifully placed, top quality single or double flowers.

What a long road it has been since the Chinese and Japanese horticulturists first became interested in the small daisy-like *Chrysanthemum indicum* and *C. sinense*, believed to be among the ancestors of our present beauties. Painstaking work by so many dedicated breeders has, over the years, provided us with the present wealth of colour, shape, form and type; and it is still continuing, so who knows what will eventually be evolved.

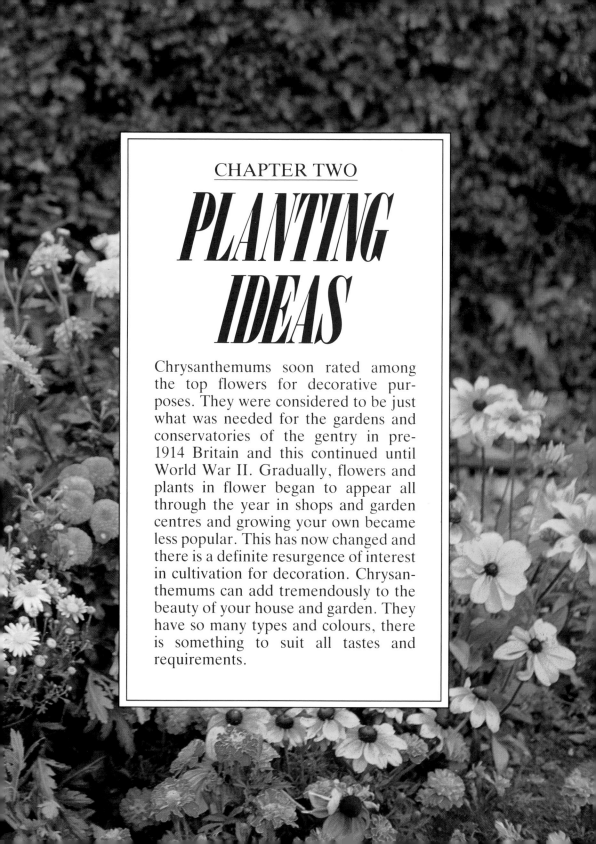

CHAPTER TWO

PLANTING IDEAS

Chrysanthemums soon rated among the top flowers for decorative purposes. They were considered to be just what was needed for the gardens and conservatories of the gentry in pre-1914 Britain and this continued until World War II. Gradually, flowers and plants in flower began to appear all through the year in shops and garden centres and growing your own became less popular. This has now changed and there is a definite resurgence of interest in cultivation for decoration. Chrysanthemums can add tremendously to the beauty of your house and garden. They have so many types and colours, there is something to suit all tastes and requirements.

In recent years there has been a tendency to treat the chrysanthemum as a hobby plant for exhibitors at flower shows. This has led to emphasis on growing methods which will produce blooms or sprays of near perfection, however time consuming they may be. It can also be argued that as the exhibitor is more concerned with flower quality, less attention has been given to developing the plant's robustness. It is natural, but not necessary, that the flower has been the overriding concern. There are still many types and variations of chrysanthemums available which are ideal for garden decoration or home beautification and with a minimum of fuss on the part of the grower.

It is worth mentioning that when I use the word 'variety' I am doing so because it is understood by most gardeners to mean a particular kind with its own colour, form and habit of growth. In fact few of the chrysanthemum plants we grow are botanical varieties and none of the commonly grown ones we are considering. A variety is a naturally occurring subject but our garden and greenhouse ones are produced horticulturally by plant breeders. They should therefore be known as cultivars. In this book I shall use the shorter commonly understood 'variety'.

'Planting Ideas' has an interesting connotation. One person's dress or colour of clothes may be considered ideal, but to another it can be awful. How do we overcome personal preferences?

Consider first the subject we are growing. The extremes are perhaps the giant or mop-headed Large Exhibition needing experience, care and a greenhouse to produce well. At the other end are the pretty bushes made by the early garden Charms known as Suncharms, with their hundreds of daisy-like flowers that can be planted in a garden bed and simply left to grow. Between those extremes we have a very wide range of colours to choose from, different flower shapes, plant habits, time of flowering and demands on time and experience. There is truly something for everyone and it is simply ideas which matter.

DECORATING WITH POT-GROWN CHRYSANTHEMUMS

Chrysanthemums can be satisfactorily grown either in the open ground, to bloom from late summer until the hard frosts in late autumn or early winter, or in containers which allow flowers either in the open or in the house or conservatory and thus extend the flowering period to winter. It is simply a matter of planning; the varieties are available.

First you have to decide for what purpose you would like to grow your chrysanthemums. Is is just for garden beauty or for cut flowers for the house? Do you want plants in containers which you can move indoors for their flowering period? Are you able to spend time

Garden pompons and sprays growing in containers with geraniums on a terrace.

on them, treating them as a hobby or interest, or do you only have limited time to give to growing them? All these factors should influence your choice.

Should you decide to follow the idea of container growing, the plants will have to be grown normally as set out in Chapter Four, and can be earlies or lates. For use in decorative schemes between late summer and autumn, the various garden-flowering types are needed. After that late-flowering greenhouse varieties come into their own. Greenhouse-flowering varieties can be grown by commencing in mid-spring and providing sheltered accommodation for flowering from mid- to early autumn. This can consist of a polythene or other suitable cover placed over them where they stand or moving them into a conservatory, light shed or sheltered corner. You must prevent frost from damaging them and you need to keep plenty of air movement going to avoid fungus attacks. A bit of experimentation should soon provide the answer.

□ HOME DECORATION

A Suncharm growing in a pot is an ideal plant to brighten your room. It can be used just as you would a hydrangea or a fuchsia and in fact if you have a suitable space to make a small display in a corner, there is much to be said for actually using all of these together. A background of fuchsias perhaps 60 cm (2 ft) or so in height with two Suncharms, one on each side, and a pot of garden pompons in the centre, colour matched, can be quite beautiful. Given sufficient room, you might even like to

add another colour or two and some green growth in the form of ferns. Maidenhair ferns are easily purchased at garden centres and so long as they are not kept in hot dry conditions, are quite successful in the house. There is of course no end to the variety of other plants which can be displayed with chrysanthemums in this way. Choosing the right colours is important, either to produce contrast or a single overall tone. I love to see a white or yellow chrysanthemum as a centrepiece for other plants, and surrounded by the greenery of either greenhouse or hardy ferns the display can be truly beautiful. There is of course no reason why a pot in bloom should not be used on its own; if it is placed on a stand in a suitable container it can make a display in itself.

Whether you use a single plant as a specimen, or chrysanthemums as part of a larger piece, it is best not to place them in direct sunlight during the summer months as this can cause scorching of flowers and foliage and dry the plants out too often.

CASCADE CHRYSANTHEMUMS

I am particularly fond of Cascade chrysanthemums, as these lovely waterfalls of tiny single flowers are truly fascinating. They can be grown as a sheet of flower 1.5 m (5 ft) long and 60 cm (2 ft) wide or, as they are in Japan, trained into shapes representing almost anything you like, from hearts to fans. The result can be used in a conservatory, in the house or even in a sheltered part of your garden when there is a spell of reasonable weather in the autumn. This is one of the advantages of pot grown plants: they can easily be placed in a suitable position and just as easily moved again. They also allow you to have plants in good flower all the time because, as they fade, you just keep changing them.

At shows in Japan, I have seen some truly breathtaking displays of chrysanthemums which could well be repeated on a smaller scale here, perhaps in a conservatory, or even a room with sufficient space. You would need, say, three Cascades trained to normal waterfall shape, a couple of late Charms to put between them, and some disbudded blooms and spray varieties at a height of about 1 m (3.5 ft). In Japan they would set the flowers around a suitable sized model of a rustic bridge or water wheel, but there are many garden ornaments used in this country which are just as appropriate, including old stone containers and statues. If you have the time and space to set up a display of this kind, you will find it compelling and creative, because you are truly building a living picture. You need to pay attention to composition, colour scheme, contrasting shape and textures and it is sheer artistry.

The above can of course be scaled down to suit your space and need not be as comprehensive. Think of one Cascade. There must be a place in your house where it would enhance the situation. Perhaps in the hall placed near to the stairs. Or on a pedestal or small table so that its foliage just clears the floor. By using a suitable colour – light shades for a dark corner, for example – it will really brighten up the place and, if

you wish, it can be left there and will last in full flower for three weeks, or even longer.

This application is also suitable for a living room where, placed in a corner opposite to the window, it can look lovely. If you have room around your house for two or three, I am sure you would be delighted with the results.

BONSAI CHRYSANTHEMUMS

Another fascinating type which enthralled me in Japan is the bonsai chrysanthemum. This beautiful little work of art needs little room and can if necessary be grown without a greenhouse. It is a real craft job and with other types of plant increasingly being used for this method there is an upsurge of interest.

Bonsai does need finishing in a suitable sized container and one which will add to its quaint appeal. A plant evenly covered with flowers on a low table in the corner of a room will give a truly oriental touch to your home decoration and they can be used in association with other kinds of bonsai plants. Those readers who are already conversant with producing bonsai beauty with other plants may like to try an arrangement of chrysanthemum bonsai flanked on each side with those dark green junipers or pines and, raised at the back, a maple in its glorious autumn orange. There are many other schemes which could also be tried. I feel sure the delights of this type of decoration will soon be widespread.

If you really want to go exotic with the orientals, try a small Cascade (say the result of a spring rooting) in white, used as a waterfall placed between rocks

(tufa if preferred), giving the effect of a mountain stream. Dwarf bonsai pines could be placed strategically at the top and a cream-coloured Charm plant at the bottom, to act as a stylized pool – quite a Japanese touch!

Bonsai chrysanthemums can be utilized so effectively with other forms of bonsai plants that the limit can be only one's ideas. A background of bonsai conifers in the form of a grove of perhaps six trees, fronted by bonsai chrysanthemums with pompon-type flowers, is another suggestion for forming a fascinating landscape picture in miniature.

Bonsai chrysanthemums growing on driftwood.

CHRISTMAS DECORATIONS

More traditional decorative pieces can be put together for Christmas. In a corner of the room stand either a late-flowering disbudded plant with several blooms on it or a Large Exhibition, grown later struck (rooting in early spring), one flower per plant in crimson. At each side place a Christmas spray variety of orange bronze, strategically place a few yellow mini mums in the centre and intersperse these with *Sola-*

num capsicastrum (winter cherry) plants with those beautiful orange berries offering contrast of shape and texture and enhancing the autumn colour.

In fact mini mums, rooted late so as to bring them into bloom for Christmas, can be an ideal room decoration. At a height of about 20 cm (8 in), they take so little room and can be placed in association with solanums, poinsettias, *Rhododendron indicum* and so many other houseplants available at that time. Dwarf pot chrysanthemums, for example, will make a solid centrepiece for them. Colour schemes can be decided from individual choice.

Talking of colour, we have not yet considered those lovely green chrysanthemums and their uses. Without artificial day-length control by blacking out, they will flower during late autumn at a height of 1 m (3.5 ft) and can be grouped together surrounded by adiantum (maidenhair) or *Asparagus densiflorus* 'Myers' (asparagus fern), to excellent effect. I would suggest, however, that you make a few experiments with 'Green Nightingale', 'Greensleeves' and some lilac and pink colours such as 'Mary Poppins', Charm 'Ringdove' and single varieties such as 'Hedgerow' or 'Party Frock' – green and lilac set each other off beautifully. Try with it one or two suitable sized plants of that lovely *Asparagus densiflorus* 'Myers' fern, one of my favourite foliage plants.

Another foliage plant which contrasts very well with chrysanthemums is *Chlorophytum comosum* (spider plant). A mature plant placed in front of a Charm in full bloom, with its trailing offsets hanging down to the ground, makes quite a spectacular piece in either its green or variegated form.

Some of the lovely palms which are available in garden centres are also excellent foils for pot grown dwarf chrysanthemums. Early pompons, early and late Charms, mini mums, can all be beautifully displayed in this way.

DECORATION WITH CUT CHRYSANTHEMUMS

We have not yet considered chrysanthemums used as cut flowers for house decoration. The traditional vase with four or five sprays or disbudded blooms can look beautiful, especially with a few trails of complementary *Asparagus sprengeri*. If you're lucky enough to own a vase of red bronze, try a piece or two of berberis with red berries.

A plant whose foliage I have found ideal for setting off chrysanthemums is the hardy fern, *Dryopteris filix-mas* (male fern), which grows extensively in many woods and hedges. A few of the beautiful fronds cut and placed either at the back of a bowl or among the blooms have real impact. The fan shape of the leaves is a perfect foil for the round chrysanthemum bloom and it does seem to be suitable for using with any colour.

A note of caution about ferns. When handling them avoid breaking the easily-damaged tip, which can quite ruin the look of the plant. Choose intact, undamaged fronds and handle them carefully. It may also be worth mentioning that you are not allowed to wander through private woods, cutting ferns without permission. Instead, why not grow some of your own? They like a moist, shady but reasonably drained position, such as in front of a north-facing wall or fence where it is often difficult to fill with other plants.

□ GARDEN DECORATION

The same questions need to be answered when deciding which chrysanthemums will best suit your garden. They can be used as individual pieces to make a focal point or as part of a larger display as a contrast to other garden plants.

About the only situation where chrysanthemums do not do well is under trees and shrubs. They receive neither sufficient water nor food in that position and it is to be avoided so far as growing the plants is concerned. However, if you are able to grow them in pots and sink them into the ground just for flowering this does not apply and they can be attractive in any situation, provided they are protected from strong wind. This is harmful to chrysanthemums, so you need to site them carefully in relation to windbreaks such as shrubs, trees and hedges.

If you have the time and inclination, instead of actually sinking them in their flowering place, make use of the fact your plants are in containers and therefore in mobile form just to decorate a particular conservatory, corner or piece of garden. They can be stood in place for a special occasion and taken back to their growing place as soon as you wish – used, in fact, in much the same way as pot plants inside the home. If you want to, you can replace them with other pots

every day or every week to give you a change of impact and scene. Just think of a batch of 20 pot-grown chrysanthemums of different colours and types used in this way. The possibilities are fascinating.

The early chrysanthemums come into their own in autumn when so many other plants are waning, if not over. Therefore, if you are thinking of using them as part of a collection of mixed plants, think first at what stage the others will be. For example, will they be in flower or will they perhaps be providing autumn colour? Consider the overall colour. Is the foliage massed or standing out? Is it dark or a light background? It is not much use putting a dark-coloured bloom against a dark background, whereas a yellow will stand out and become a focal point. Should the overall appearance be silvery, then pinks and purples come into their own. You are building a picture just as if you were an artist painting it or a photographer taking it.

So long as you are using container-grown plants they can be placed anywhere and changed easily. In fact they have great advantages over planted subjects except for one thing; they need to be watered often and fed occasionally. If you have to carry water a long distance to reach them, this can be a daunting factor.

THE PATIO
Troughs or ornamental pots are excellent for growing chrysanthemums. A patio with two or three of these to provide decoration can look delightful.

They can of course be chrysanthemums on their own or, if you wish, mixed with other plants. An early Charm surrounded by lobelia or alyssum is most attractive; alternatively use a taller early spray variety or even one of the shorter disbudded kinds as the main subject and surround these with edging plants such as the dwarf *Begonia semperflorens* (fibrous-rooted) or a pink alyssum where you are using a pink, purple and white scheme.

It is best to use a fairly short season of growth, say plants rooted in mid-spring, so that the final pot size can be about 18 cm (7 in). This gives you more plants and more types per square metre of available space than if you used larger pots containing larger plants resulting from a longer growing season.

Early disbudded blooms and sprays will reach a height of about 1 m (3½ ft) and Suncharms 45 cm (18 in), making a dome of bloom up to 38 cm (15 in) or more across. They can be positioned and altered so that maximum use of shape and colour can be maintained. In the warmer summer months they need frequent waterings and this should be kept in mind. An appropriate source of supply is advisable!

DECORATION WITH PLANTED CHRYSANTHEMUMS

If you prefer to use chrysanthemums planted and growing in the chosen spots because of the ease of maintenance, then other factors arise for consideration. You need to choose types which will suit the surroundings when in bloom, so consider the position in relation to trees, shrubs and the sun. Make sure you have suitable soil with sufficient food available and that it is not waterlogged.

Among the loveliest garden-grown chrysanthemums are Suncharms. These flower from late summer until mid-autumn, make mounds of colour, need little attention and are easy to grow. Imagine a garden path from gate to door with a mass of colour on each side, the additional benefit of a scent of honey, and visited by butterflies on this account. Planted in May, they need no staking or disbudding and provided the ground is in good heart, extra feeding is not essential. By using either one colour throughout, one colour each side or alternate colours along the rows, you can get a lovely display. This can either be used on its own or allied to other suitable chrysanthemums or other plants.

Suncharms are low growing, only about 30–45 cm (12–18 in) high and admirably suited for association with taller plants such as standard roses or fuchsias. The colour scheme can be thought out in advance using either matching hues or contrasting colours. Depending on the width of the bed, you can place the chrysanthemums between the roses, in a double row each side of them or perhaps in batches round each one. If you decide on edging plants such as annuals, choose those which will remain in flower through into the autumn such as ageratum. This ensures the

full benefit of the colour scheme.

A variation of this approach would be to use taller bushes of chrysanthemums provided by the garden spray varieties, as a foil perhaps, in place of some or all of the roses. You may like to consider this for a planting scheme in other parts of the garden. Tall disbudded blooms or sprays at the back, cushion Suncharms in front and extended to include other plants such as marigolds and tagetes. Use contrasting colours, shapes and heights to create interest. Consider using the taller spray varieties on each side of the doorway so that you have a lead-in to a focal point. Use the colour contrast to enhance this, for example a row of bronze and orange along the path

Above. *An exhibition of some of the different types of chrysanthemums grown in Japan.*

Opposite. *The use of Suncharm chrysanthemums to extend the period of flower in a bed of annuals.*

leading to taller yellow sprays by the doorway, or variations of this using purple and pinks with a white door feature. Should you decide on the latter colour scheme, try echeverias along the edge of the beds. They contrast very well alongside chrysanthemums, in colour and shape, and are decorative from early summer until mid autumn.

HERBACEOUS BORDERS

Most gardeners choose to have an

herbaceous border; at its best, there are few things to equal it in a garden. However, the plants give their best display in mid-summer, after which they have fewer flowers. From late summer onwards the Michaelmas daisies are at their best, just when the chrysanthemum comes into its own.

Clumps of three or four chrysanthemums are better than separate plants and in the herbaceous border space should be left for suitable varieties. Taller sprays and disbudded blooms should be at the back, in front of the tall Michaelmas, making a triangle say 1m (3½ft) wide at the back narrowing down to a point at the front using shorter Spartans, and pompons which can be treated as herbaceous plants and left in over winter, Spartans being fully hardy and many of the poms moderately so. A few patches set out in this way will enliven the bed during the autumn days.

CHRYSANTHEMUMS AND WATER FEATURES

Pompons come into their own when there is a water feature such as a pool. They are tough, plentifully flowered and long lasting. Used with a background of hardy ferns or reeds at the edge of a pool, they are lovely. Compact and only about 30cm (12in) high, they make a mass of colour. They must not be planted as part of a bog garden but otherwise are very tolerant of soil conditions.

HARDY CHRYSANTHEMUMS

The hardy Spartan chrysanthemums have many uses in the garden. Once established they can truly be left in the

ground to grow again next year, all having been subjected to at least four winters in the open ground before being first offered to the public. They are ideal for edging around tall plants or shrubs; sharing the herbaceous border; used on a rockery; filling the odd dull corner, and many similar situations.

Consider Spartans in the centre of a bed surrounded by suitable annuals such as lobelia, heliotrope, the smaller types of marigold, with *Chrysanthemum parthenium* (golden feather) as an edging. Plant this alternately with lobelia then inside this a ring of marigolds and the Spartans as a centrepiece. This will provide flowers from early summer to mid autumn.

They can also be bedded out in front of or around ornaments or statues. Here, use the ornament as a focal point, say at the end of the garden and against a dark background if possible; subjects such as yew or ivy over a stump, or a dwarf-growing conifer, come to mind, using the Spartans to add that colour contrast which catches the eye.

CHRYSANTHEMUMS ON THE ROCKERY

Spartans are excellent plants for suitable spots on the rockery. They need more soil space than many of the true rock plants but will be ideal where a pocket can be prepared between two rocks. Work into the soil some peat or leaf mould to provide humus, and a suitable

Garden flowering pompons and sprays growing in containers and used for a temporary 'special occasion'.

depth of root run so that hot sunny weather will not cause too much drying out and they will grow well. Good drainage will help chrysanthemums to survive wet winter conditions.

Early garden pompons are also very attractive in these spots, although they would probably have to be planted afresh each spring. Most rockeries are sparsely flowered from late summer on and chrysanthemums used in this way can give an extended period of colour and beauty.

If you have a bed of about 3 m (10 ft) at the top of a bank or rockery, you can exploit both texture and colour by planting a *Yucca flaccida* and a *Yucca filamentosa* (Adam's needle) at each end and filling between with early pompons, Suncharms or, if you want to leave them permanently, Spartan varieties. The difference in foliage colour against the grey-green of the yuccas, and the contrast in outline between their respective leaf shapes and the dwarf-growing chrysanthemums set off by the tall creamy flowers of the yucca, make a striking composition. They both benefit from the well drained position, although in a hot dry summer the chrysanthemums would gain from a top dressing of peat and may need water.

CHRYSANTHEMUMS IN ANNUAL BEDS

Another use in conjunction with annuals is to have your bed laid out with chrysanthemums at each end and also in the middle in three larger beds, joined by a narrow bed of annuals between. I like to see the two end beds planted with taller spray earlies at the back, fronted by Suncharms or pompons and edged at the front with lobelia or alyssum. The joining bed of annuals looks particularly effective if backed by *Cleome spinosa*, which gives height, and then patches of marigolds, antirrhinum (snapdragons) and those lovely bedding geraniums which are now available in many colours. For a front, I love a clump of three plants of the pale *Lobelia erinus* 'Cambridge Blue', three golden feather and three of the dark blue 'Crystal Palace' lobelia, continuing these alternately right down the bed.

If you wish to give some variation to the chrysanthemums, the middle bed can be planted with a different colour scheme from the ends and all shorter-growing Suncharms or pompons. Placed about 45 cm (1.5 ft) apart, they make a real mass of flower by autumn.

BEDDING IN LAWNS

Another excellent use of chrysanthemums is in lawn beds that have been cut out and the soil made suitable by working in manure or compost and fertilizer during the winter. If you have a greenhouse or conservatory in which you can grow on a yucca, bed this into the centre in early June and surround it with Suncharms and pompons. They will provide both colour and form for long periods and once again the contrast in foliage is attractive, with the exotic appearance of the yucca complemented by the more homely chrysanthemum foliage. All the plants can be lifted before frost damage occurs.

Another summer bedding plant which

makes a wonderful centrepiece to a bed of chrysanthemums in a lawn is abutilon. Again, it is not safe to plant it out before frost danger is past, but two or three beds with yuccas and abutilons will create an exotic atmosphere in the garden – not quite subtropical but getting towards it.

If you have a suitable wall space with a bed in front, try a background of ivy with chrysanthemums. The ordinary ivy with its dark green leaves makes a perfect foil for the lighter-coloured chrysanthemums in yellow, white and pink; while the variegated 'Goldheart' is beautiful backing for darker pinks, purples and crimsons. Both subjects attract insects and butterflies and this gives an added appeal in a warm corner.

Do you have a summerhouse in your garden? If so, you have an ideal foil for a few chrysanthemums. First, plant a couple of climbing roses, one on each side in a colour which appeals to you. If you decide on a crimson and a yellow, train these to cover the top half and roof of your summerhouse. Make a bed around the house about 60 cm (2 ft) wide and plant disbudded types or sprays, or both, spaced out about 1 m (3½ ft) apart; in front of and between these, site three shorter spray varieties and in front again a row of Suncharms. Your summerhouse will look beautiful and a real focal point in the garden.

USE IN FLORAL ART

I am not qualified to propound on floral art but I have always found it fascinating and naturally am interested when use is made of chrysanthemums as the main subject or in harmony with other flowers. Once in my younger days a trained florist was demonstrating the use of blooms of one of the mop-headed 'big as your head' varieties and with a deft twist and loop of two leaves of the yellow iris and a base of fern leaves, she transformed it into a beautiful ornamental picture. It can be done; it should be done more often.

I have seen some beautiful pieces using perhaps three blooms, suitable foliage to cover the base, and a tortured twisted twig set up in a dish of sufficient width to balance the height. Nowadays, with the availability of Oasis blocks, you can so easily put blooms just where you want them; it matters not whether it is the neat circular shape of the ordinary flowers, or the completely different quills, spoons and spiders. The range of colours and forms makes most ideas possible.

Chrysanthemums can also be displayed with containers of fruit, using the fruit as a base for suitably positioned flowers. The lighter spray types are particularly beautiful for a Harvest Festival.

Chrysanthemums are particularly suitable for church decoration to enhance special occasions. They are happy in cool conditions and tend not to be adversely affected by dull light. Besides the traditional cut flower use, Charms, Cascades and other pot grown varieties are beautiful. Choose those which flower when you require them and grow them for the occasion. Remember, dark colours do not show up in dark corners.

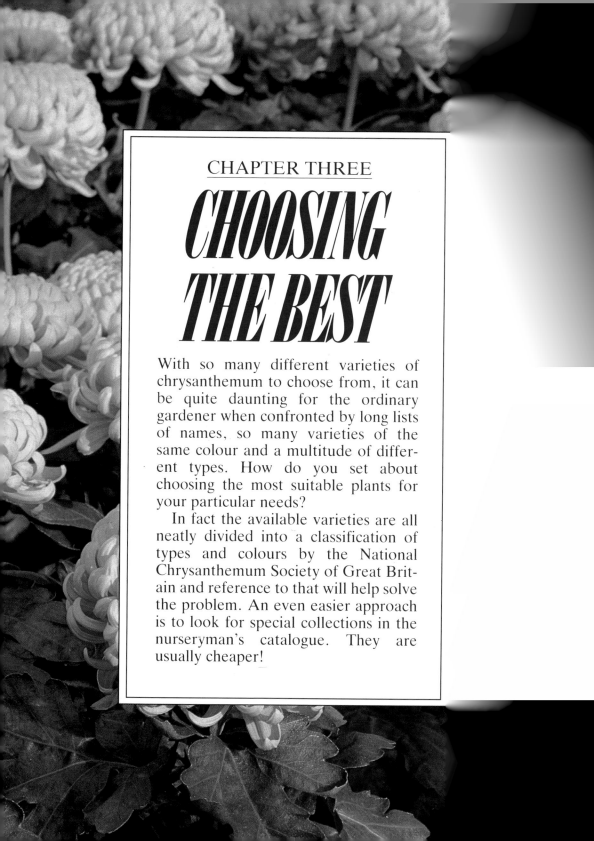

CHAPTER THREE

CHOOSING THE BEST

With so many different varieties of chrysanthemum to choose from, it can be quite daunting for the ordinary gardener when confronted by long lists of names, so many varieties of the same colour and a multitude of different types. How do you set about choosing the most suitable plants for your particular needs?

In fact the available varieties are all neatly divided into a classification of types and colours by the National Chrysanthemum Society of Great Britain and reference to that will help solve the problem. An even easier approach is to look for special collections in the nurseryman's catalogue. They are usually cheaper!

It is important when ordering chrysanthemums, that you choose the best varieties for your purpose. There are so many different types, each with unique characteristics, and it is very easy to choose wrongly. If, for example, you are interested in providing cut flowers for the home, which also require a minimum of attention, it is pointless to choose from those which are perhaps tip top exhibition varieties but need careful cossetting to flower them properly.

What then are the guidelines for selecting from among the many different types, those varieties which will suit your purposes?

If you study a specialist chrysanthemum grower's catalogue, you will see a list of names under each group heading, all having accompanying key letters and numbers alongside the name e.g. 'Red Woolmans Glory' 7a. This means that 'Red Woolman's Glory' is a large-flowering (a) single (7) which blooms under glass in late autumn; alternatively, 'Pennine Salute' (29d) is a garden-flowering spray (not requiring disbudding) single (d). Sometimes there is also shown a colour code attached to each variety – DP is dark pink, LY is light yellow, for example.

The above system is primarily intended for the exhibitor who enters blooms in specified classes at a show under the appropriate section heading, but it does also enable the general gardener to pick out his preferences.

You will find all suppliers offer collections of plants under various type headings – garden-flowering sprays for instance – and it is usually easier and certainly cheaper for the non-specialist to take advantage of these offers.

The National Chrysanthemum Society is responsible for registering and classifying all new varieties. They must be submitted and so registered before they can be used at chrysanthemum shows in Britain. Here then is set out the main structure of this classification system, together with some of the varieties under each heading which are available at the time of writing. Chrysanthemums, as a whole, are divided into three groups; late-flowering, covering those in bloom in late autumn to mid-winter; mid-season to late autumn; and early-flowering, which bloom from late summer to mid-autumn or until the frost damages them. Each group is further subdivided according to its habit, flower type, and colour.

INDOOR-FLOWERING (GREENHOUSE) VARIETIES

Section 1.	Large Exhibition (both incurving and reflexing).
Section 2.	Medium Exhibition (both incurving and reflexing).
Section 3.	Exhibition Incurved (large-, medium- and small-flowered).
Section 4.	Reflexed Decoratives (large–, medium- and small-flowered).

'Green Satin'. One of the few truly green varieties – beautiful in artificial light as a cut flower.

Section 5.   Intermediate (incurving) Decoratives (large-, medium- and small-flowered).

Section 6.   Anemone-Centred (large-, medium- and small-flowered).

Section 7.   Singles (large-, medium- and small-flowered).

Section 8.   Pompons (*a*) True pompons (*b*) Semi pompons.

Section 9.   Spray varieties (*a*) Anemone-centred (*b*) Pompons (*c*) Reflexed (*d*) Single varieties (*e*) Intermediate (incurving) (*f*) Spiders, quills and spoons (single or double) and other types.

Section 10.   (*a*) Spiders (*b*) Quills (*c*) Spoons which are disbudded to bloom.

Section 11.   Any types not fitting the classifications set out.

Section 12.   (*a*) Charms (*b*) Cascades.

OCTOBER-FLOWERING (GREENHOUSE AND GARDEN) VARIETIES

Section 13.   Incurved varieties (large- medium- and small-flowered).

Section 14.   Reflexed varieties (large- medium- and small-flowered).

Section 15.   Intermediate (incurving) varieties (large-, medium- and small-flowered).

Section 16.   Large October-flowering.

Section 17.   Singles (large-, medium- and small-flowered).

Section 18.   Pompons (*a*) True pompons (*b*) Semi pompons.

Section 19.   Spray varieties (*a*) Anemone-centred (*b*) Pompons (*c*) Reflexed (*d*) Single varieties (*e*) Intermediate (incurving) (*f*) Spiders, quills and spoons (single or double) and other types.

Section 20.   Any other types not already covered by the classification.

Section 21.   Not yet used for classification.

OUTDOOR-FLOWERING (GARDEN) VARIETIES

Section 22.   Early garden flowering Charms.

Section 23.   Incurved (large-, medium- and small-flowered varieties)

Section 24.   Reflexed (large-, medium- and small-flowered varieties).

Section 25.   Intermediate (incurving) (large-, medium- and small-flowered varieties).

Section 26.   Anemone (large-, medium- and small-flowered varieties).

Section 27.   Single (large-, medium- and small-flowered varieties).

Section 28.   Pompons (*a*) True
                pompons (*b*) Semi
                pompons.
Section 29.   Spray varieties (*a*)
                Anemone-centred (*b*)
                Pompons (*c*) Reflexed
                (*d*) Single varieties (*e*)
                Intermediate (incurving)
                (*f*) Spiders, quills and
                spoons (single or double)
                and other types.
Section 30.   Any other types not
                already covered by the
                classification.

In addition to the preceding classes there is a colour classification of white, cream, yellow, pink, salmon, bronze, red, purple and other colours not specified in the foregoing.

INDOOR-FLOWERING (GREENHOUSE) VARIETIES

SECTION 1. LARGE EXHIBITION

This group is primarily of interest to the exhibitor, and in fact is a type which is often taken up once he has gained experience on the other sections. It is called Large Exhibition, and until the 1940s they were always known as Japanese chrysanthemums, 'Japs' for short. This type needs much care and knowledge to obtain top class exhibition blooms. However, when this is achieved it is a magnificent product: huge mops as large as your head; a thousand or more petals curling and interlacing into a bloom 23 cm (9 in) across and 30 cm (12 in) deep. They make a fine display of great interest at the larger shows when entries call for six, nine or 12 blooms in a class.

The basic method of cultivation applies of course but there are a few 'extras' needed. These have to be learned through experimentation and experience. It used to be said by the smitten that you were not a complete grower until you could produce good Large Exhibition blooms. Be that as it may, if you can succeed with these, you certainly are a top grower; it is a target to be aimed for. Many say that they are purely for exhibition purposes and have no decorative value. I don't agree with this: three blooms in a tall vase will grace any room and invite comment. They are worth the effort.

You need to have a greenhouse with heat available to cultivate Large Exhibitions. Use the basic cultivation as set out in Chapter Four. The cuttings, however, need rooting from early to mid-winter, according to the variety, and this has to be learned. Once rooted, they should be kept in cool open conditions with sufficient heat to keep out the frost, a minimum of 3°C (37°F) will do. In mid-summer reduce the shoots to two and sometimes to one later in the season.

Stopping and timing are extremely important with this section. The aim is to produce buds for disbudding to one per shoot in late summer. Some varieties are stopped once to bloom on the first side shoots (first crown buds); others twice, thus producing buds on the second set of side shoots (second

Above. *'Tang'. A most attractive example of the late flowering Charm type.*

Opposite. *'Shirley Primrose'. An established Large Exhibition variety of top class quality.*

crown). Stopping – that is pinching the top 2 cm (1 in) off a shoot – is carried out between early spring and early summer, according to the variety. There are guidelines on this procedure available from the British National Chrysanthemum Society, and the specialist chrysanthemum nurseries also give recommendations in their catalogues.

Whether you grow on first or second crown, and when you time the buds, can alter the number of petals produced and thus the form of the flower. The aim is to produce blooms which are at their best in late autumn when the late shows are held. A cut bloom will last in a cool room for three weeks or more for decorative purposes. Plants grow in height from 1 m (3.5 ft) to 2 m (6.5 ft), according to variety, and a well grown plant will produce large dark green leaves which will add considerably to its beauty.

There is another method of producing blooms for house decoration with this section. The cuttings are rooted in early spring, potted into 8 cm (3 in) and then into 13 cm (5 in) pots in which they are flowered. They are then allowed to grow without a pinch and produce one bloom on the main stem. This gives you a dwarf plant about 60cm (2ft) high and can be very decorative in the home.

There are of course certain varieties which are currently leaders in the exhibition world and the wise grower uses these as a base while experimenting with others, both new introductions and old favourites. I would suggest you begin with any of the following:

'Duke of Kent'

Strong growth producing large foliage to a height of about 1m (3.5ft). When reduced to the normal one or two blooms per plant the flower is large, up to 23cm (9in) across and at least as much in depth. The long interlacing petals fall neatly into shape. The colour can vary from near white on the earliest flowers to pink on the later ones. There are also yellow and pink sports (mutations) with the same habit and flower type.

'Gigantic'

Just about the largest of the giant section and grown extensively by all exhibitors. The size of the very solid bloom is outstanding, up to 25cm (10in) across and the same in depth. Besides the chestnut bronze original variety there are three sports, amber, silver and golden. However, these are very close to the parent variety and unless you are intending to exhibit at shows they are not necessary. Height 1.2m (3.5ft).

'Jessie Habgood'

A large pure white with extra long petals making a bloom up to 30cm (12in) deep. Somewhat smaller foliage

than the two previously mentioned varieties but similar in habit of growth. Height about 1.2m (3.5–4ft).

'Phil Houghton'

The bronze bloom is made up with wide petals which curl and interlace making a near ball-shaped flower up to 20cm (8in) across and of even greater depth. Very solid. Not quite such attractive foliage as some others but an outstanding bloom when grown well. Height about 1.2m (3.5–4ft).

'Pink Duke'

A pink sport (mutation) from 'Duke of Kent'. The colour varies from blush pink in the earlier blooms to medium pink in the later ones. The habit and height otherwise similar to the parent.

'Shirley Primrose'

This variety produces a massive bloom up to 30cm (12in) deep with a broad square top. The shiny petals curl and interlace to build an outstanding flower. Large, medium-green foliage on a plant primarily for exhibition but majestic in its decorative value.

SECTION 2. MEDIUM EXHIBITION

This section is closely allied to Section 1 and the needs, so far as cultivation is concerned, are similar, the main difference being that in Section 1 size is of primary importance and shape and quality slightly less so. In Section 2 form and neatness take precedence to some

'Pink Gin'. One of the late flowering spray types which are so lovely for decoration.

'Rynoon'. A really beautiful example of the single flowered late spray chrysanthemums.

extent over size, which is why you see exhibits of smaller but similar type blooms. They are, in fact, quite distinct varieties.

There is a greater colour range in this section because some of the strong crimsons and purples seem genetically linked to the smaller size and these are mostly classified in this section. If you are inclined towards using this type for house decoration, then it is well worth starting with Section 2 rather than Section 1.

Among those varieties of this class of chrysanthemum which are most widely grown are:

'Amethyst'

A rich attractive colour with very neat blooms up to 18 cm (7 in) across and at least as deep. A very lovely bloom carried on plants up to 1.2 m (4 ft) high with large deep green leaves.

'Cossack'

A truly striking scarlet crimson with neatly laid long petals building into a bloom of great beauty. It makes a plant 1.2 m (4 ft) high.

'Green Goddess'

An unusual colour which can be described as sea green. It is particularly attractive when used in conjunction with flowers of deep pink to lilac colour and can make a lovely centrepiece to a large arrangement of chrysanthemums. It has a slightly weaker root system than most of the others in this section and so must not be overwatered during the earlier part of its growing season. Once established, however, it grows normally. Height of this one is up to 1 m (3.5 ft).

'James Bryant'

The rich crimson colour of this variety has made it a favourite for many years. A beautifully neat reflexing bloom of long substantial petals making it strikingly attractive. Two blooms per plant, carrying healthy medium green foliage. Height 1.2 m (4 ft).

'Lundy'

A lovely white variety, having the usual solid, reflexed bloom of the section. A foil for the stronger deeper colours. Medium size foliage on plants up to 1 m (3.5 ft) in height.

'Majestic'

This has maintained its popularity for many years and is still one of the widely grown varieties in the section. Neatly laid long reflexed petals make a bloom of great solidity and an attractive amber colour. There are also sports (mutations) in yellow and red. The height of the plant is about 1.2 m (4 ft) and it carries large deep green leaves.

'Seychelle'

A lovely pink bloom of great substance. This is deservedly popular with the exhibitor, but has plenty of other admirers because of its beauty. Deeper than it is wide, the flower has great appeal. Height up to 1.2 m (4 ft).

SECTION 3. EXHIBITION INCURVED

Section 3 comprises those beautiful near-perfect ball-shaped incurved types, again flowering in late autumn under greenhouse conditions. They need the basic chrysanthemum cultivation, rooting in late winter or early spring and potting on into mid and final pots, but they do not require as much feeding during the growing season as Section 1 and 2 varieties. The aim is for a perfectly formed top and a round base giving the ball-shaped bloom. If you allow them to produce too many petals they become irregular and lumpy and thus lose value when being exhibited. The usual procedure to lessen the petal count is to grow them on second crown, that is pinching them twice, usually in mid spring and again in early summer. The aim here is to produce quality blooms with size being secondary.

Exhibition Incurved are the favourites of many growers and are extremely popular. The height when in flower varies between 1 m (3.5 ft) and 2 m (6.5 ft) and it is therefore important to select types which will fit comfortably in your greenhouse. Heat is beneficial during the flowering time in late autumn, but not absolutely essential. Air movement provided by fans or ventilation is also advantageous, to prevent damping caused by fungus attack.

These varieties are widely grown for exhibition and decoration alike:

'Fairweather'

This is excellent for exhibition purposes but also makes a beautiful cut bloom for decoration, or even as a pot plant when up to five blooms can be grown instead of the normal three. Beautifully incurving. The colour is medium pink but there are several sports (mutations) of different colours available, including 'Bronze Fairweather' and 'Oyster Fairweather'. An added attraction is its height of 90 cm (3 ft).

'John Hughes'

A classic true exhibition incurve in both shape and quality. Beautifully ball-shaped blooms with hardly a petal out of place. All other incurved are compared with it for neatness. Pure white in colour, medium sized blooms on a plant carrying the normal three or four flowers. Height 1 m (3.5 ft). It has a yellow sport (mutation) which is equally attractive.

'Robeam'. So useful for cut flower decoration; the late sprays are recommended as part of any collection.

'Lakelanders'

A most attractive shining pink colour with near perfect ball-shaped blooms on strong stems with small foliage. This is a recent addition to the section and has immediately attracted attention. Height 1.3 m (4.5 ft). An added bonus is that it can also be flowered satisfactorily in mid autumn if planted out in the garden.

'Megan Woolman'

Very pure white blooms of ideal exhibition quality. Slightly broader petals than the previous variety and well worth its place in any collection. Height 1.3 m (4.5 ft).

'Shirley Sunburst'

A beautifully formed exhibition incurve of large size and excellent quality. An attractive yellow colour. Although of larger size it retains the shape and neatness needed for exhibition. Height 1.3 m (4.5 ft).

'Yellow Shirley Imp'

A rich yellow of near perfect form and shape. The petals are rather wider than most of its section and this gives it a shining quality. Most attractive. Medium sized foliage on a plant up to 1.2 m (4 ft) high.

Sections 4 and 5 are termed reflexed and intermediate decoratives. These are the types normally grown for cut flower decoration in the house. A greenhouse or conservatory is necessary and although artificial heat is an advantage since they bloom from late autumn to early winter, it is not essential. Protection from frost is needed and this, of course, becomes more difficult without artificial heat as mid-winter approaches. The bubble-type plastic sheeting now available for fixing inside the glass makes a considerable difference, and it also helps to save on fuel bills.

SECTION 4. REFLEXED DECORATIVES

Reflexed decoratives are those which have petals drooping downwards from a button centre. They are available in a range of lovely colours and are the mainstay of blooms for decoration. These days they are available in florists' shops throughout the year but under natural conditions are autumn- and winter-flowering. Their cultivation is straightforward and they vary in height from 1 m (3.5 ft) to 2 m (6.5 ft). A good plant will carry five blooms of reasonable size and quality.

The following can be recommended:

'Christmas Wine'
This is of particular value for cut flower decoration because its normal flowering time is in the winter. An unusually rich ruby wine colour, it has been popular for many years. The habit of growth is neat and strong. Height 1.2 m (4 ft).

'Dorridge Velvet'
A very rich crimson colour with beautiful velvety petals, this makes an impact straight away. The neat habit of the plant with its small dark green foliage adds to its attractiveness. This is one I particularly like and ideal where space is scarce. Height 1.5 m (5 ft).

'Glorietta'
The medium powder pink of this variety

is beautifully displayed by slightly rolled petals which provide a flower that is hard and very resistant to damage. It is a fine cut bloom and lovely for house decoration. A compact habit of growth also helps. Height 1.4 m (4.5 ft).

'Shoesmith Salmon'
Another variety which is of value because its normal flowering period is early to mid-winter. Neatly laid petals make an attractive bloom of mid-salmon colour. Excellent for decoration and long lasting. Height 1.2 m (4 ft).

'Tom Stillwell'
There is a scarcity of real yellow varieties in the reflexed decorative section and this is a pleasing variety of primrose yellow. The bloom is comprised of quite long, neatly reflexed petals and looks attractive. Medium green foliage. Height 1.4 m (4.5 ft).

'West Bromwich'
A large, well-reflexed bloom which is very popular with exhibitors and wins many prizes. There are also several sports of different colours. It can be used for cut flower purposes but may be on the tall side for a small greenhouse. Early struck cuttings produce plants up to 1.6 m (5.5 ft); later ones are dwarfer.

SECTION 5. INTERMEDIATE DECORATIVES

These used to be called incurving: that is to say, they are between the true

'Roblaze'. A handsome example of the double flowered late spray section.

incurved bloom and the reflexed one. The petals curve upwards and inwards to the top but they do not make the perfect ball shape of the incurved. Many people prefer them for decoration.

One point worth mentioning is that incurved and intermediates have a smaller colour range than reflexed types because they present the underside of the petals to view. The colour of the reverse side of petals is usually white, yellow, bronze or silver, whereas the reflexed show the top of the petals and in the true chrysanthemum colours.

Cultivate this section as recommended generally. Height between 1 m (3.5 ft) and 2 m (6.5 ft). They will carry five blooms.

'Kingfisher'. The late Charm section is a valuable decorative piece during winter.

It may be of interest to mention that wherever height and bloom quantity is stated for the disbudded bloom types, it is assuming that they are rooted at the normal recommended time. If you wish, you can root later with many varieties, grow fewer flowers per plant with stopping adjustment and you will get good blooms on shorter plants. You get this result if, say, you grow a decorative variety which is rooted in mid spring, potted into an 8 cm (3 in) pot and then in early summer put three plants into a 20 cm (8 in) pot missing out the 13 cm (5 in) size.

Recommended varieties for this section include the following:

'Corngold'
A beautiful corn yellow colour. Blooms of good size and with a shine which makes it particularly attractive. A neatly closed incurving top adds to its appearance. One which I particularly like. Height 1.4 m (4.5 ft).

'Greensleeves'
One of a small number of green chrysanthemums. A most attractive cut flower of sea green colour. The slightly incurving petals shine and particularly enhance lavender and pink colours displayed with them. The green varieties tend to be a little less robust in

'Ryflash'. A truly beautiful example of the dainty single flowered late spray varieties.

growth than other colours and in general need less watering. Height 1 m (3.5 ft).

'Hazel McIntosh'
A truly beautiful, shining rich buttercup yellow, the loosely incurving form enhancing the richness of colour. A really striking variety of strong growth with medium-sized dark green foliage. Excellent for home decoration. Height 1.3 m (4.5 ft).

'Sheila Morgan'
Broad shining petals build up into a

most attractive golden bronze.
Excellent for cut flower purposes. The flower is attractively incurving at the top and of a pleasing near-ball shape. Long lasting and very lovely medium green foliage on a compact plant. Height 1.3 m (4.5 ft).

'Skaters Waltz'

A lovely medium pink colour with long incurving petals building a large bloom. Excellent for house decoration, it goes particularly well with 'Greensleeves'. Medium green foliage. Height 1.2 m (4 ft).

'Snowshine'

Valuable as a winter flowering variety when blooms are scarce. A pleasing incurving form, a really pure white set off by deep green foliage. Height 1.2 m (4 ft).

'Violet Lawson'

A beautiful large-sized white bloom which can be flowered mid to late autumn. Although popular with the exhibitors because of its quality, it may be difficult for small greenhouses owing to its height of 1.5–1.8 m (5–6 ft). Apart from this, it is a really lovely variety in this section.

SECTION 6. ANEMONE-CENTRED

This type is in appearance a single chrysanthemum with a cushion of short tubular petals instead of the daisy eye as in the normal single. It is excellent for home decoration and some very attractive colour combinations are provided when the cushion is different from the petals. In earlier years these were ex-tremely popular and much in demand. More recently they seem to have gone slightly out of fashion, which I think is a pity.

The cultivation of this type is similar to that of decorative chrysanthemums and the flowering height can be varied too.

Recommended varieties include the following:

'Bridget'

A lovely powder pink with a pronounced cushion of the same colour. Medium-size foliage. There is also an attractive bronze sport from it. Height 1.2 m (4 ft).

'Cloudbank'

Pure white, both ray florets and cushion. Very beautiful for floral art. Strong growth. Height 1.3 m (4.5 ft)

'Epic'

The ray petals are an attractive lavender colour while the cushion is orange brown. Most pleasing under artificial light. Height 1.2 m (4 ft).

'Raymond Mounsey'

Cinnamon bronze, both cushion and ray petals and a somewhat larger flower than the others. Height 1.5 m (5 ft).

'Red Admiral'

A bright bronze red with a hint of gold in the cushion. Compact growth. Height 1.3 m (4.5 ft).

It should be said that these are not as readily obtainable from nurserymen as

An attractive example of the late flowering Fantasy type.

other types mentioned and you may have to search for them. Those which are offered are mainly anemone spray types, but they can be disbudded if preferred.

SECTION 7. SINGLES

These daisy-eyed blooms with perhaps four or five rows of petals and that lovely centre of green changing to yellow are a delight. As well as being ideal for floral decoration in some beautiful colours, they can be grown for exhibition with disbudded blooms up to 13 cm (5 in) across. Their cultivation is as set out generally and they will carry seven or eight blooms per plant with a height of 1 m (3.5 ft) to 2 m (6.5 ft). They also have an additional benefit in that they give a honey scent which is not only pleasant but attracts insects too.

Recommended varieties include the following:

'Choirboy'
A medium-sized bloom of clear white with very neatly laid petals. Compact growth. Height 1 m (3.5 ft).

'Hedgerow'
Another of medium size and a lovely pink colour. Strong growth with small foliage. It also has sports (mutations) of varying bronze colour. Height 1.2 m (4 ft).

'Lovely Charmer'
A beautiful amber bronze which seems

'Goldplate'. Strongly recommended as an easy growing variety for cut flower in the autumn.

to shine. Very neat and a good habit. 1 m (3.5 ft).

'My Love'
A most distinctive colour including both apricot and salmon shades. With its medium-sized blooms of perfect form, this variety has been successful both for exhibitors and as a cut flower for decoration. Strong growth and small foliage. Height 1.2 m (4 ft).

'Woolmans Glory'
This variety and its several sports of yellow, red and crimson has dominated the large-flowered single section for a generation, and has not yet been surpassed. Strong growth and dark green foliage complete the picture. Height 1.3 m (4.5 ft).

SECTION 8. POMPONS

This is an interesting and very old section designated Pompon chrysanthemums or, as most people call them, 'Poms'. They are button heads of short petals and have long-lasting qualities. Although one of the earliest chrysanthemum introductions, the greenhouse-flowering varieties in this section are now less popular than they were, regrettably I feel. The chrysanthemum has such a wealth of variation in type, and the range in Britain does not compare favourably with those of other chrysanthemum countries. No doubt they will eventually return to favour, but unfortunately there are few sources of supply at present. The height is about 1 m (3.5 ft) and they carry up to 10 blooms per plant.

Varieties which were deservedly popular included:

'Baby'. Yellow.
'Dresden'. China pink.
'Ethel'. Bronze.
'Golden Climax'. Rich golden yellow.

SECTION 9. SPRAY VARIETIES

In recent years this section of chrysanthemums has increased considerably in popularity. It is of course the mainstay of the chrysanthemum supply through florists' shops and is used extensively for house decoration – deservedly so. It has also made terrific strides in the exhibition world, where a class of entries in this section can cause much admiration and interest.

At this point we are considering the late autumn to early winter greenhouse-flowering varieties. The flower-type covers all the sections of ordinary blooms available, the basic difference being that a spray – that is, a stem with a number of side flowers on it – is produced without disbudding, which is done with the one-bloom-per-stem type. They are rooted and grown on as is recommended basically and are both popular and easy to grow. They will carry up to five sprays per plant and are up to 2m (6.5ft) in height. Because of this, a slight variation of cultivation has been devised to provide dwarfer plants. This of course is a great advantage when you have limited height in your greenhouse; in fact I doubt if this section would have developed in quality and popularity the way it has, without this development.

Cuttings are rooted in early summer or, if you are buying from a nursery, plants will be sent then. Using one of the suitable mixtures they should be potted either one plant into a 13cm (5in) pot or three plants into a 20cm (8in) pot. Pinch out the tips in mid-summer and later remove any weak shoots, leaving about three per plant. No disbudding is necessary. By this method you will produce those lovely sprays of bloom on a plant about 1m (3.5ft) in height, which is so much more manageable.

This section includes almost all the types of chrysanthemums available as disbuds. The most popular are the single flowered section 9d and double reflexed ones 9c. There are a few examples of spray intermediate 9e but I personally do not think they are as attractive in spray form as the double reflexed ones. Spray anemones 9a are quite beautiful and among my favourites. There are also some very appealing spiders, quills and spoons in section 9f (see below). These quilled petal varieties are a pleasant variation. I think the pompons are, if anything, more attractive in spray form 9b than when disbudded. There are a number of very beautiful varieties among the sprays. The best are:

'Pink Gin'
Deep pink double flowers of great beauty. Height 1.2m (4ft).

'Robeam'
Double flowers of a rich buttercup yellow colour set off by dark green foliage. Height 1.2m (4ft).

'Chaffinch'. This Suncharm variety is an example of chrysanthemums used with hardy ferns in the garden.

'Roblaze'
Deep red blooms of a slightly incurving type making a pleasing spray of flowers for vases. Compact habit. Height 1.2 m (4 ft).

'Romark'
Clear white compact blooms making an excellent and luminous display. Height 1.2 m (4 ft).

'Ryflash'
A lovely rich crimson single flowered spray of great delicacy. Height 1.2 m (4 ft).

Above. *'Peter Rowe'. An established variety much used for both cut flower and exhibition purposes.*

Opposite. *'Early Red Cloak'. This has graced our gardens for many years and is still an excellent cut flower.*

'Rynoon'
A delightful powder pink single flowered spray. Very lovely and of compact habit. There are several colour sports of this variety which are also excellent for cutting or border decoration. Height 1.2 m (4 ft).

SECTION 10. SPIDERS, QUILLS AND SPOONS

To further consider the types of disbudded blooms, we will look at spiders, Section 10a, quills 10b and spoons 10c. These three are sometimes called 'fantasies'. The petals are of tubular form of varying length and thickness. They are widely and beautifully grown in Japan where they have many in lovely pastel colours. I am hoping, once again, that their popularity will increase here, together with those other unusual types, the thread-petalled and paint-brush varieties. The spoons which are included in this group are in fact quill-petalled ones which split open to make a small spoon-shaped end. In Britain we do not allow rings to be placed under these sections when they are exhibited, whereas in Japan they are so displayed in order to evenly distribute the petals, which can be up to 25 cm (10 in) long. Whether or not you prefer the formal approach or the informal one, these are very lovely blooms and quite entrancing. The height is 90 cm (3 ft) to 1.8 m (6 ft) and up to five or six blooms per plant are produced.

I am particularly fond of these:

'Green Nightingale'
Long quilled petals of a rich green make this an unusual variety either as disbudded or spray. Height of this variety is 1 m (3.5 ft).

'Quill Elegance'
Pure white rolled quill petals set off by a yellow to green centre in the younger blooms. Strong in growth. Height 1.2 m

(4 ft) for late spring-rooted cuttings. The rich yellow sport of this variety is also attractive.

'Rayonnante'
Magenta pink. One of the oldest of the quill petalled varieties which together with its sports, bronze, white and yellow, is still popular. It can be flowered in a sheltered place in the garden in mid-autumn, but is usually grown in pots for late autumn blooms. Height 1.2 m (4 ft).

SECTION 11. ANY OTHER TYPE

Another group of windowsill chrysanthemums, of great value where space is at a premium, are the 'Mini-Mums' (Section 11). They carry beautiful starry, spoon petalled daisy flowers on plants 18 cm (7 in) high. They need a short season of growth and can be flowered at any time of the year. Their greatest use is probably early winter. Cuttings rooted in early autumn and potted in mid-autumn will bloom naturally, giving invaluable beauty at that dark time of the year.

Pot them in a soilless mixture into 8 cm (3 in) pots and leave them to flower. If necessary some suitable high potash type of tomato food can be given in the later stages. A minimum night temperature of 10°C (50°F) will be needed for bud formation. If flowering is wanted during the period early spring

'Cloth of Gold'. A variety which has stood the test of time as a cut flower and decorative chrysanthemum.

Above. *'Dorridge Crystal'. A recent introduction of mine which has already made an impression for garden and exhibition.*

Opposite. *'Flo Cooper'. Basically an exhibition type which has been successfully used for decoration.*

to early autumn, it is necessary to black out the plant to give short days and initiate buds. In practice, this simply means putting a light-tight box over the plant from around tea time to breakfast time, commencing about three weeks after potting. They flower about 12 weeks after potting up and will stay in bloom for up to five or six weeks. Recommended varieties are as follows:

'Charisma'
White ray petals with a yellow anemone centred cushion.

'Mary Poppins'
A rich pink spoon-petalled single.

'Red Pixie'
Another spoon-petalled single with a golden eye.

'Thumbelina'
A yellow spoon-petalled single.

SECTION 12. CHARMS AND CASCADES

If you require something more unusual for decoration in the home, why not grow some late flowering Charms? In bloom from late autumn to early winter, these are delightful. They provide a dome-shaped cushion up to 1 m (3.5 ft) across, covered with daisy-like flowers in many colours. They need no stopping or unusual methods of cultivation and just naturally grow in this form. The treatment is similar to that given for pot-grown chrysanthemums, beginning with an 8 cm (3 in) pot and ending with a 20 cm (8 in). It is also useful that you can either have a big 1 m (3.5 ft) diameter plant by rooting it in late winter or early spring or, if you prefer it because you do not have sufficient space, you simply root it later – any time up to late spring – and your plant will be proportionately smaller and can be flowered satisfactorily in a smaller pot. Recommended varieties are as follows:

'Bullfinch'. Rich shining crimson.
'Kingfisher'. Pretty cerise colour.
'Morning Star'. Rich yellow.
'Ogmore Vale'. White.
'Ringdove'. Pretty candy pink.
'Tang'. Bright tangerine.

Cascade chrysanthemums (Section 12) are a truly beautiful type which were once very popular in Britain. They are less widely grown at present, perhaps because they take up considerable space at flowering time, but there can be few flowering plants which will give as much satisfaction in full bloom. They can be grown into a cascade of small flowers tumbling down from a pot anything up to 2 m (6.5 ft) long and 1 m (3.5 ft) wide. Truly magnificent.

Their cultivation is basically similar to other chrysanthemums in as much as a rooted cutting is potted into an 8 cm (3 in) pot in mid- or late winter and grown on in the normal way. Where it differs from the basic method is in that you need to pinch and train the plant throughout the growing season. It may also need a 25 cm (10 in) pot for final potting. I have seen it at its best in Japan, where magnificent specimens are displayed in the parks and shrines in late autumn. Here of course we have to bring it into a greenhouse or conservatory before frost can damage it. Cascades are still grown by some of our parks and it is available as seed from some of our main seedsmen. Feeding is needed more than with ordinary types of chrysanthemums as the plant carries such heavy growth. At later stages feed at least once a week with the usual chrysanthemum fertilizer.

As soon as the plants have become established in their mid or final pots, stand them on the ground and insert a cane 2 m (6.5 ft) in length, angled to about 45°. Place the pot so that the cane points to the north, as this will cause the resulting shoots to grow out towards the sun and in one direction, thereby producing a plant facing one way. Each side

shoot is pinched at about every second joint through the growing season until early autumn and the main shoot is tied to the cane. If necessary, additional canes can be put in place to secure the side shoots. At housing time the plant is carefully taken into a greenhouse or conservatory and placed on a shelf of suitable height to allow it to hang down in a cascade. The cane or canes are removed and the tip of the plant secured to the ground. The normal flowering period is late autumn to mid-winter. Named varieties are not readily available from nurserymen although they can be obtained. If seed is used it should be sown in the normal way in late winter, with bottom heat of 15°C (59°F).

SPECIMEN PLANTS

Among the unusual types of chrysanthemums which are specialist products is the specimen plant. There are a few decorative types which can, if grown correctly, produce plants from a single cutting which carry up to 300 blooms on a 120 cm (4 ft) wide plant, each bloom being of normal size and quality and all out together. This is achieved by experience and a considerable expenditure of time and patience from the beginning in early winter until flowering time in late autumn. I will not go into details here but refer anyone interested to the *Chrysanthemum Manual* available from the British National Chrysanthemum Society. Suffice it to say that the initial plant

'Pennine Gambol'. A beautiful example of the Anemone-centred section which is ideal for decoration.

has to be stopped by pinching out the tip of the main shoot during mid-winter and the side shoots stopped again about three times, the last time being mid-summer. In this way, and by adequate potting on to a final 45cm (18in) diameter pot, the magnificent plant up to 120cm (4ft) across is produced. Two commonly used varieties for this purpose are:

'Princess Anne'. A reflexed decorative.
'My Love'. A single.

BONSAI CHRYSANTHEMUMS

There is another kind of late autumn-flowering chrysanthemum which is widely grown in the U.S.A. and Japan but hardly known in Britain, and that is the bonsai chrysanthemum. It can be brought to flowering in either one or two seasons, and is similar in form to the various other kinds of bonsai plants we know.

In Japan this type has a great significance relating to folklore and emotion. The various types and shapes are given titles and meanings and they are grown in various forms such as 'upright', 'cascade', 'plantation' (a group of plants in one container) and many others. The type of growth is quite natural to the varieties used and they are liberally flowered with small single or double blooms, evenly spaced over the plant. Provided you have time and patience, you can have a finished plant in bloom in 10 to 15 months. They don't need much space of course, but you do need a frost-free greenhouse or a suitable conservatory.

The cutting is rooted in mid- to late autumn in a normal rooting medium or, if preferred, a basal shoot with its roots is cut from an old plant and is ready to grow on. Potted into a 5cm (2in) pot, it is ready for the 'off'! Training and shaping begins when about 10cm (4in) high which will be in early spring: the tip of the shoot is pinched off and at the same time any large leaves from further down are removed as they would be out of keeping with the small-leaved ideal of the developing plant. Later flushes of leaves will be smaller.

As the plant grows, a soft wire is used to guide the branches into the correct shape for the type you have decided on. This is done either by wrapping it round and then bending it in the direction you want, or used as a peg to hold down a branch. The shoot tips are pinched as necessary to develop the 'tree'. They are grown in ordinary pots, potted on as necessary to provide enough food and lastly into the display container, when root pruning can be done if necessary to restrain their growth.

The aim is to grow bulky main stems which become like small tree trunks, with short side shoots evenly spaced carrying blooms spaced over the entire plant. This summary is of course very incomplete, but again more detailed information can be obtained from the NCS *Chrysanthemum Manual*. I do recommend that you attempt this delightful kind of chrysanthemum. At present it is hardly known in this country but there is stock available from a few sources. Hopefully more will be introduced.

OCTOBER-FLOWERING VARIETIES

In the classification system of the NCS, the next main grouping is October-flowering, that is to say, varieties which will flower in mid-autumn, outside in the garden in some cases but under cover for some of the larger blooms and when grown for exhibition. For our purpose we will approach them from the decoration and cut flower angle.

This section is comprised of similar types to the previous late autumn and mid-winter classification. The cultivation can be either in pots or planted into

'Bronze Fairie'. An ideal garden pompon variety which is excellent for bedding.

the ground. If the latter, then some temporary cover may be needed at flowering time to prevent weather damage.

There are many excellent varieties available and I am particularly fond of the following:

SECTIONS 13. INCURVED AND 15. INTERMEDIATE VARIETIES

'Brideshead'
13. A pretty pale pink incurved bloom. Height 90 cm (3 ft).

'Goldplate'
15. A delightful golden amber semi-reflexed bloom. Strong growth. Height 90 cm (3 ft).

'Karen Riley'
15. An attractive bronze incurving bloom. Height 120 cm (4 ft).

'Shirley McMinn'
15. A recent introduction. Large flowers of medium pink colour. Height 105 cm (3.5 ft).

SECTION 14. REFLEXED

'John Riley'
Deep red. Height 105 cm (3.5 ft).

'Riley's Dynasty'
A truly rich deep pink colour with shining petals. Height 90 cm (3 ft).

OUTDOOR-FLOWERING (GARDEN) VARIETIES

In NCS terminology an early-flowering chrysanthemum is one which flowers naturally in the open garden by early autumn. For our purposes, it will be a variety which can be flowered in the garden until the frost damages it beyond repair, probably either early or late autumn.

SECTION 22. EARLY GARDEN-FLOWERING CHARMS

These chrysanthemums are the Sun-charms, which I have already mentioned. They are my favourite garden chrysanthemums, require a minimum of attention and give a maximum of enjoy-ment. They have a type of growth which produces lovely cushions of bloom and flower from late summer until the hard frosts in mid- to late autumn. Cultivation is similar to that already set out.

Rooted cuttings are planted out in a garden bed in late spring and grown on. No supports are required. There is no stopping or disbudding to be done and they will produce a mass of single daisy blooms in beautiful colours which are very weather resistant. In addition they provide copious pollen which, with its honey scent, attracts bees and butterflies. It is delightful on a sunny autumn afternoon to have this patch of colour and its insects in your garden.

Charms grow to about 40 cm (15 in) in height and can reach 60 cm (2 ft) in diameter; real beauty. They are available from seed through some of the main suppliers and as named varieties from specialist chrysanthemum nurseries. As garden plants they are high on my list. Besides this, they are wonderful when planted in containers to brighten a patio or conservatory. Used in this way they can be grown in any of the normal chrysanthemum composts. Named varieties available and recommended include:

'Chaffinch'
Covered with pink starlike flowers.

'Goldcrest'
With bright yellow single blooms.

'Redwing'
A rich scarlet red which also has the characteristic of making early blooms soon after planting out and then

growing on into a bush for flowering at the normal time. It is also dwarf in habit, reaching about 30 cm.

'Skylark'

A lovely biscuit amber, a little taller than the others at a height of around 45 cm (1.5 ft), but still the characteristic cushion form.

'Wagtail'

A clear white of large growth making a most attractive plant and a foil for the other stronger colours.

There are no sections of garden chrysanthemum which relate to the greenhouse-flowering Large Exhibition or Medium Exhibition, Sections 1 and 2. They begin with the true incurved form and designated Section 23. These varieties which need to be disbudded to one bloom per stem and three stems per plant for exhibition quality can be grown up to five stems per plant satisfactorily but do need disbudding. They are very popular for home decoration and have good lasting qualities when cut. They are best supported with a cane and tie. Cultivation is straightforward. I can recommend:

SECTION 23. INCURVED

'Alison Kirk'

A lovely pure white of true incurving form. Dark green leaves on a sturdy plant. Height 1 m (3.5 ft).

'Dorridge Dream'

A rich medium pink colour with neatly laid petals forming a ball shaped bloom. Sparse growth. Height 1 m (3.5 ft).

'John Statham'

A rich buttercup yellow colour. A beautifully ball-shaped true incurved bloom. Sparse habit and strong stems. Height 1 m (3.5 ft).

'Peter Rowe'

A leading variety both for cut flower decoration and exhibition. Neatly incurved of a bright amber yellow colour. Height 1 m (3.5 ft).

SECTIONS 24 AND 25. REFLEXED AND INTERMEDIATE

As with later-flowering varieties, the classification sets out reflexed and intermediate sections. They can, from the point of view of growing and use, be considered together. They should be disbudded to one bloom per stem and three to six stems per plant according to whether you need large or medium blooms. The colour range is rather greater in the reflexed varieties than the intermediate (or incurving) ones, but both have their respective beauty. Staking and tying are needed, and cultural needs are as set out for general growing.

There is a large number of varieties to choose from and apart from personal preference, the main distinctions to look for are weather resistance and height. If you live in a windy area such as high altitude or near the coast, then dwarfer kinds give best results. In any case some attention to natural windbreaks can pay handsome dividends, and a strategically placed patch of trees or shrubs can be invaluable. Among my favourites in this highly desirable section are the following.

'Bambi'

A lovely apricot bronze reflexed bloom which can be grown to quite a large size if required. Medium green foliage. Height 1 m (3.5 ft).

'Cloth of Gold'

An excellent garden or cut flower bloom. Grows freely and makes a mass of double reflexed blooms of rich yellow from late summer. Height 1 m (3.5 ft).

'Early Red Cloak'

Rich crimson scarlet reflexed flowers of medium size suitable for decorative purposes. Height 1 m (3.5 ft).

'Evelyn Bush'

A long established variety which has stood the test of time. Clear white incurving blooms of great appeal. Strong habit of growth. Height 1.2 m.

'Flo Cooper'

A large incurving of rich clear yellow. Strong habit. This has been popular for many years. Height 1 m (3.5 ft).

'Gambit'

Deep cerise reflexing blooms of large size. Has been a top exhibition variety for many years. Strong growth. Height 1.2 m (4 ft).

'Grace Riley'

A beautiful bronze reflexed bloom which has great appeal. Has proved itself over many years. Height 1 m (3.5 ft).

'Marlene Jones'

A beautiful incurving bloom of clear yellow colour. Strong stems and compact habit. Height 1 m (3.5 ft).

SECTION 26 AND 27. ANEMONE-CENTRED AND GARDEN SINGLES

These are two sections of chrysanthemums which are still included in the NCS classification, although they have lost their former popularity and have now almost gone out of cultivation. In my opinion a pity, although it may be that there will eventually be a resurgence of interest. I hope so.

The anemone-centred flowers can have most attractive cushion centres and when disbudded, have blooms up to 10 cm (4 in) across. The varieties which are still available, even if rather scarce, include:

'Pennine Gambol'

An anemone-centred single of a most attractive pink colour. Height 75 cm (2.5 ft).

'Pennine Oriel'

White with a cream anemone centre, spray or disbud. Most attractive. Height 90 cm (3 ft).

'Sally Ball'

Bronze anemone-centred single making a lovely cut flower. Height 90 cm (3 ft).

'Sunblaze'

Anemone-centred and a bright yellow colour. Height 75 cm (2.5 ft).

The disbud singles have, I believe, all but disappeared, with the exception of a few in amateurs' gardens.

'Salmon Fairie'. A lovely sport from Fairie which should be in all garden collections.

SECTION 28. POMPONS

Fortunately, another ancient but very useful section, the early-flowering pompons, Section 28 is very much with us, although in recent years there have been few additions to the range, bred among others by the Johnson brothers of Tibshelf in Derbyshire. Luckily, the varieties they introduced have not deteriorated and are still available and worth including for garden decoration.

They produce a lovely mass of blooms on bushy plants from 20cm (8in) to 45cm (18in) high. They can be used as cut flowers, for which they have excellent lasting qualities, or for garden decoration in beds. The small spray type flowers with compact button blooms are very weather resistant and few of the varieties require any artificial support. Just the kind of chrysanthemum needed when there is no time available to cosset the plants. These together with garden flowering Charms and Spartan hardy chrysanthemums, are ideal when you prefer flowers to fussing! The best varieties now available are:

'Bronze Fairie'
A bright cinnamon bronze with very neat flowers. A compact bush in form. Height 30cm (1ft).

'Cameo'
Beautiful little button-shaped blooms of pure white. Free-growing. Height 45cm (1.5ft).

'Denise'
Rich yellow, strong growth making a real cushion of colour. Height 45cm (1.5ft).

'Fairie'
The original pink in this group of colour sports. An ideal garden decoration plant. Height 30cm (1ft).

'Salmon Fairie'
A delightful salmon sport from 'Fairie', with the same compact free-growing form. Height 30cm (1ft).

SECTION 29. SPRAY VARIETIES

The next main section under NCS classification is 29, spray varieties for early garden flowering. This type has increased in popularity to a considerable extent in recent years and in my opinion quite rightly. The spray chrysanthemums available in the shops throughout the year are late blooming ones brought into flower artificially. These early garden sprays enable the ordinary gardener to produce similar ones quite naturally, without artificial aids.

There is a great range of bloom type; something to suit everyone. You can produce sprays which have a mass of bloom of the reflexed or intermediate incurving type; there are singles of great beauty; not to forget the quills, spoons and spiders which can be grown. The colour range is wide, in fact for garden decoration and cut flower, suitable spray varieties are a must. They bloom from late summer to the frost and will carry up to seven sprays of suitable quality per plant. Most varieties are around 1m (3.5ft) in height and therefore need supporting. They are worth the trouble.

In addition to the above, if any varieties appeal particularly to you, you can if you wish disbud a few plants to one bloom per stem and thus obtain blooms of types such as anemone-centred, which are not readily available otherwise; and there is quite a scope for experimenting here to find which of your favourite sprays will also produce attractive blooms when disbudded. How to choose the most suitable ones? The main chrysanthemum specialist nurseries have good illustrations and offer collections, so I can recommend starting there. Get your base collection in this way and then gradually extend it. You will enjoy the search and trialling of new kinds too.

Among the many varieties of which I am particularly fond are the following selection:

'Anna Marie'
Beautiful white double flowers freely produced on strong stems. Height 1 m (3.5 ft).

'Carol Moonlight'
A really lovely double-flowered variety used both as an exhibition spray and for cut flower decoration. Cool, clear pink in colour. Height 1 m (3.5 ft).

'Lilian Hoek'
A well tried variety excellent for garden decoration. Compact in growth. Double flowers of attractive bronze colour. Height 90 cm (3 ft). There is a similar red sport.

'Marie Taylor'
Double flowers of rich purple colour. Excellent for home decoration. Compact habit and strong stems. Height 1 m (3.5 ft).

'Muriel Foster'
A delightful white single flowered spray which is very popular. Free flowering. Height 1 m (3.5 ft).

'Pennine Jade'
Rich tangerine, a striking colour with dainty single flowers freely produced. Height 90 cm (3 ft).

'Pennine Tango'
Attractive single flowers of bronze colour. Very good for cut flower decoration. Height 1 m (3.5 ft).

The following two groups, if used for exhibition purposes, are entered in their respective sections, according to their type of flower.

KOREAN AND RUBELLUM VARIETIES

Another very useful group for garden decoration are the Korean and Rubellum varieties. While not completely hardy they are considerably so. They are bush type plants producing a mass of spray blooms but taller than the Charms and more similar to the garden-flowering spray varieties mentioned earlier. They vary in height from 45 cm (18 in) to 1 m (3.5 ft) and are ideal for using in the garden with a chance of surviving the winter. The flowers are tough and not easily damaged by bad weather. They are not as generally available now as they were in earlier years, but they can still have a valuable purpose in the garden. The following are among the best varieties:

'Belle'
A bright red single making a dwarf plant

suitable for garden decoration. Height 60 cm (2 ft).

'Doris'

A bright golden bronze semi-double flower. Long strong stems excellent for home decoration. Height 90 cm (3 ft).

'Hazel'

Pretty spoon petalled blooms of a golden bronze colour. Most attractive. Height 90 cm (3 ft).

'Joan'

Lovely sprays of peach coloured semi-double flowers on stems suitable for cut flowers. Height 90 cm (3 ft).

'Moonlight'

Handsome sprays of double yellow blooms. Height 60 cm (2 ft).

HARDY GARDEN VARIETIES

So far all the various garden types which we have considered have needed lifting in the autumn after flowering, or at least needed some protection from the winter weather. There is, however, a group recently introduced which I have developed over the last 15 years by cross breeding early spray varieties with some old cottage garden hardy chrysanthemums which I gathered from about the country as available. These are at an early stage of development, but already some very attractive ·varieties have appeared and have been made available under the title 'Spartan'.

It is a slow business breeding and selecting them, because each batch of seedlings has to be planted into the open and left for several years in the ground to prove their hardiness before they can be used as further parents for cross pollinating. I decided on a period of four years for this hardiness test, because during that time they are likely to experience most types of winter weather and if they survive they can then be considered safe to offer as hardy perennial chrysanthemums. A point worth mentioning is that chrysanthemums are at least as susceptible to winter wet as to cold, and those planted in a well drained situation are much better able to survive than those in wet heavy conditions. This should always be borne in mind when planting in your garden.

At the present time the varieties on offer are for spray blooms for garden decoration or cut flower, although some could be disbudded if larger blooms are required.

All the Spartans increase the number of their shoots the longer they have been planted, forming a bush of flower from basal shoots which appear each spring. After a few years they can be split into smaller pieces and replanted.

'Spartan Bronze'

With a height of 60 cm (2 ft), produces a spray of single blooms of a bright orange bronze with a yellow ring around the daisy eye and is quite striking.

'Spartan Flame'

Grows to 60 cm (2 ft) and has an attractive spray of double blooms, scarlet crimson in colour and is one which if preferred could be disbudded to one bloom per stem. In fact any of the Spartans could be grown as dual purpose varieties disbudding some blooms for cut flower decoration and leaving others for garden display.

'Spartan Orange'

An attractive amber orange with compact double flowers. It is particularly attractive grown as a bush type. Height to 60 cm (2 ft).

'Spartan Pink'

Another double spray variety with medium pink coloured blooms is excellent for cut flower. Height 60 cm (2 ft).

'Spartan Rose'

This variety has most attractive deep pink single sprays of flower and is lovely as a garden display subject. At a height of 60 cm (2 ft), it is easily manageable (in fact, in most situations the Spartans would not need staking and tying to support them).

'Spartan White'

Sprays of semi-double blooms of a clear white. A foil for the other colours, or of course, may be made into a bed on its own. Being a little taller than the others, it makes good cut flowers. It reaches a height of about 1 m (3.5 ft).

'Spartan Yellow'

Produces a mass of single spray flowers of a bright yellow colour which quite light up their area and is excellent for a dull corner in the garden. Grows to 60 cm (2 ft).

SECTION 30. OTHER TYPES

Recently some very attractive bush type garden varieties from the U.S.A. have become available, which are worth considering. They should be grown in the early stages as ordinary outdoor chrysanthemums but need the tips of the shoots pinching out as they become long enough, right up until mid summer. By doing this you can produce a bush up to 45 cm (18 in) across and 30 cm (12 in) in height covered with small flowers. They are also hardy in many localities. I can recommend:

'Ginger'. An attractive light bronze.
'Goldmine'. Bright yellow.
'Remarkable'. A lovely bright red.

CHAPTER FOUR

GENERAL CULTIVATION

The cultivation of chrysanthemums has been often wrapped in mystery. The old gardener learned the hard way how to produce the results wanted and was not prepared to give away the 'secrets' of success. Thus it came to be believed necessary to produce a magic pinch of something from an old apron pocket.

Fortunately, today knowledge of cultivation methods is freely given. There are a few basic rules but apart from these you can give as much or as little time to the plants as you wish.

This chapter sets out the basic principles, and the reader can experiment with them. Some chrysanthemums need only to be planted in the garden and left to grow.

The best method to use in chrysanthemum cultivation is in many cases experience and preference. I have seen exhibition plants belonging to top growers looking quite different from each other and being treated differently. One person believes in short stocky plants grown cool and hard in the early stages, another in plants that are lush and protected. One will feed early in the season, the other believes in producing as many roots as possible and then feeding later. Some keep their plants in the greenhouse as long as they can, others put them in a frame as early as conditions allow. Temperature, watering and feeding can all be variable. The common factor among such growers is that they end up with top class blooms.

What can we learn from this? It seems puzzling but in fact, it isn't. In order to flourish, chrysanthemums need a minimum temperature of about 7°C (45°F), plenty of air, not too much water and plenty of light. In most parts of Britain protection from frost between mid-autumn and early spring is needed, and an open site with a buoyant, not too humid, atmosphere is best. Winter-flowering chrysanthemums will need protection, heat and ventilation at night to get maximum results.

So what if you are unable to provide all this? You have an unheated greenhouse or only a frame or perhaps neither of these. Does that mean chrysanthemums are not for you? Certainly not! What it does mean is that you must choose types, varieties and methods which are within your range of facilities. Chrysanthemums know how to grow, you must let them do this by giving them suitable conditions. More plants are killed by kindness, particularly in the early part of the season while they are becoming established, than by neglect.

The best methods of propagation are set out in Chapter Five. In this chapter we will assume rooted plants are available, either from your own propagation or from a nurseryman or garden centre. The plant should be about 8 cm (3 in) to 20 cm (8 in) high and with a reasonably compact set of roots and be ready for growing on. If you have purchased by mail order and your plants arrive just as you are going away for the weekend, don't worry. Check to see whether they have dried out, moisten the roots, wrap a piece of polythene around the roots and lower stem only and put them upright in a cool shady spot, protected from frost, until you return. They will be perfectly all right; chrysanthemums are tough and, apart from overwatering, it is difficult to kill them.

If you are able to give part protection in some form, you will do better to have your plants in early spring so that you can grow them on to a more advanced state before planting out. If you are unable to do this, tell your supplier that you want them to plant straight into the ground. They will then be sent in late spring. Remember that you can grow them outside in most places, without protection from mid-spring, so long as you can cover against an occasional hard frost, or have the means to move them into an outhouse or conservatory for a short time if necessary to protect them from harsh weather.

GARDEN-FLOWERING VARIETIES

First, you need to consider the garden-flowering types which bloom from late summer to the first heavy frost.

□ GROWING ON BEFORE PLANTING IN THE GARDEN

If you are able to grow them on before planting, the easiest method is to make up a box with soil or peat potting mixture and plant them firmly into that. A suitable box is about 18 cm (7 in) deep and, from the point of view of handling, about 30 × 23 cm (12 × 9 in), which will comfortably hold around 18 plants.

The mixture which you use should not be too rich. You have a choice of a traditional soil mixture, which you make up yourself, and other ready-made soil-based or peat potting composts. If the mixture is very dry, it is best to wet it and turn it over a day before you use it. After boxing, water in well and then give no more than a spray over for a few days. Extend this to a week or 10 days in later winter or early spring, if the weather is cool or wet.

Planting should be done so that the roots are just covered by compost. The box should be placed in an open situation with plenty of light, although from mid-spring a bit of temporary shade may help for a few days if there is hot sun. In general, however, the plants soon toughen up and initial flagging will cease.

The worst thing you can do is to keep watering them because they flag. Leaves wilt when the sap supply is less than the loss of water through their pores. This certainly occurs if they are too dry, but it also happens in the stage immediately after they have been planted or potted on because the roots are not yet functioning in the fresh soil, and even if it is sufficiently moist they cannot make use of it. If you keep watering, the roots become bereft of air and gradually die. If you simply spray over the foliage it minimizes the fluid loss and gradually the roots resume their work. It does however take quite a lot of nerve to withhold water from a plant when the leaves are flagging. Be comforted by the knowledge that if you withhold water plants do not die for a long while, whereas if you overwater it can happen quite quickly. A good tip is to check any doubtful plants first thing in the morning. If they are dry they will still be flagging, if they are too wet the compost will be damp and the leaves at least reasonably fresh. If in doubt do not water.

Once the plants are established and growing in their boxes, they should be kept cool and in open conditions. No artificial heat is necessary unless it is needed to prevent frost damage, and even if no heat is available sufficient covering will do. Even a couple of layers of newspaper will suffice in the spring months. As a rule no support or tying will be needed at this stage.

Planting out into the garden can be done as soon as reasonable danger of frost damage has passed. In Britain this means mid-spring in the softer western and coastal areas and late spring elsewhere. Chrysanthemums thrive in medium loam soil with a reasonable amount of humus in it. If you have light sandy soil or heavy clay soil the overriding need will be for humus. In the former, you want to increase water retention, and the latter to help drainage. *Chrysanthemums do not like their feet in water.*

□ PREPARING THE GROUND

Preparation should commence during the winter months, in fact as soon as possible after clearing the ground in autumn. All old leaves and growth should be removed to lessen the chance of disease and pest carry over, after which the ground should be dug or rotavated. The necessary humus and food base is ideally supplied by a dressing of cow or stable manure. This is not easily obtained nowadays, unless you live near a riding stable, but is worth searching out to help build a good crumbly loam. If you cannot find manure, there is a ready substitute for most gardeners – the compost heap. If well prepared and rotted to a clean crumbly consistency, the material from this spread liberally before digging will be as beneficial as farmyard manure. Do however avoid including old chrysanthemum material and any grass cuttings on which hormone weed killer has been used. The former can transmit disease and the latter could do some irreparable chemical damage that would ruin your plants. Humus not only provides basic food needs but also encourages the increase of organisms which break down the soil into a suitable condition for the plants to use. With clay soil old ashes or

similar material worked in helps to improve the texture.

Planting time is some time during the spring period, according to where you live and the danger of late hard frost. Chrysanthemums will stand a few ground frosts after planting but an air frost of a few degrees will check or damage them. Planting time moves from the south-west up the west side of Britain and then from the south-east and up the eastern side during that period. Sheltered or open conditions will of course also play a part, as will altitude. Some of the best chrysanthemums are grown in central England at altitudes of 240m (800ft), but you have to be careful with them when first planted. Similar flexibility will be necessary in other countries. Take local advice.

Preparing the ground for planting begins in early spring when a forking over or rotavation to break it down into a fine tilth is desirable. This also gives you a weed clearance at just the right time. You can now rake in a dressing of chrysanthemum or tomato-type fertilizer, according to instructions.

□ PLANTING OUT

Before planting, first water the plants so that they are well charged and will suffer the check better. Make a hole of sufficient depth to enable you to finish with the ball of soil just comfortably covered,

'Spartan Torch'. A beautiful example of this hardy chrysanthemum section which I have recently introduced. Will overwinter in the ground.

place the plant in it and firm in the replaced soil. It is advisable to put a cane of about 1 m (3.5 ft) in place during planting and tie the plant to it if it is tall enough. If you leave this job intending to do it later, your plant will almost inevitably suffer wind damage before long. A useful alternative to sticks and ties is a 20 cm (8 in) mesh of wire netting. (Plastic netting of similar mesh could be used, if it can be kept really rigid.) This can be laid on the ground and planting carried out through it, at the same time using it as a guide to spacing – 45 cm (18 in) between plants. Firm posts should be placed at each corner, up to 10 ft apart, keeping the mesh secure as it is lifted to keep up with the plant's growth thus minimizing the labour of tying (Fig. 1). Unfortunately, this may not be suitable if you are growing your plants in a border among other plants.

Water the chrysanthemums in after planting and leave them to become established. If the plants have been grown on before planting they will be fairly hard and will not suffer much flagging, unless the weather is particularly hot and dry. If this is the case, spray them over morning and evening for a day or two. Should they have just arrived from the nursery and are softer and smaller, a bit of shade for a few days would help them. Remember, chrysanthemums thrive in open conditions with plenty of light, which means they do less well in shade and under trees. Better positions will always produce better plants.

The main growing season is from planting time until mid-summer. How they are treated during this time will directly affect autumn flowering. Ex-

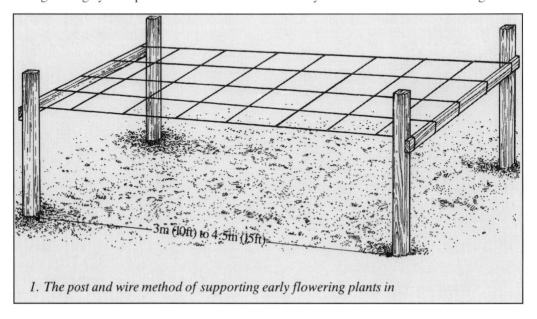

1. The post and wire method of supporting early flowering plants in

hibitors will tie them up, feed and water them, giving treatment which balances up each seasonal variation. If it is a wet summer they will produce soft growth and need little water but extra potash. A dry one will produce harder plants which can be watered and fed with extra nitrogen. What then should the ordinary gardener do to keep a balance between too much work on them and the need for good results?

If you have prepared the ground with humus or manure and worked in some suitable fertilizer before planting, there will be sufficient food available to produce good plants. The only attention needed will be supporting the plants by tying them to a cane and giving them a good soaking once or twice a week if we have one of those hot summers with a drought for several weeks. Otherwise let them get on with growing and just enjoy looking at them!

□ STOPPING AND TIMING

One of the most puzzling parts of chrysanthemum growing to most people is the frequent references made to stopping and timing. What does it mean and how on earth can it be understood?

In fact it is not difficult. When a plant is growing it will increase in height and

2. A young plant in its early stages before any natural breaks or stopping.

3. A break bud occurring naturally on a young plant.

4. *Side shoots growing after a break bud has appeared and which has eventually died away.*

First crown buds

5. *Side shoots eventually form buds which if allowed to flower are called first crown.*

produce leaves (Fig. 2). When it has a sufficient number of leaves it will produce buds and then flowers. In the case of garden chrysanthemums the main trigger for bud formation is temperature. As it gets warmer so they make buds. The usual sequence is for a bud to appear on the top of the single main stem in late spring or early summer, called the break bud (Fig. 3), and then, instead of developing into a worthwhile flower, side shoots grow from the top few leaf joints producing in this way several leafy shoots (Fig. 4). Ultimately each of these will make buds at the top and become flowers (Fig. 5).

Why, therefore, worry about stopping? If, as in many varieties, the sequence occurs so that the buds produce good flowers at a suitable time i.e. late summer to mid-autumn, there is no need to alter anything. If however, as in some varieties this sequence is going to produce blooms too late to be of any use, then it gives better results if the first break bud is anticipated by previously pinching out the top inch or so of the shoot (Fig. 6) and forcing the plant to make side shoots earlier than it naturally would, thereby bringing the flowering forward to a more suitable time (Fig. 7). In specialist nurserymen's catalogues

6. *A young plant which has been stopped by having the main shoot pinched out before a bud can form.*

7. *After being stopped the plant produces side shoots.*

you will find a key to stopping and timing and each variety which they list will have a reference to this.

What if the grower just does not want to bother with this? There are two general rules about growing chrysanthemums: either pinch out the tops of any stems not making a bud by early summer, or leave them to do it themselves and enjoy the flowers whenever they are produced. Stopping and timing is not an exact science; apart from anything else it varies with the geographical location and the time the plants were rooted, so unless exhibition blooms are required do not worry about it. On the other hand, if you are intending to exhibit or want to produce top class exhibition blooms, you have to be more precise. But there are plenty of adequate books on the subject and many chrysanthemum societies to help you.

□ THINNING OUT

Another point to decide as the plants grow larger is how many stems to leave per plant. It is natural that the more blooms there are per plant the smaller they will be. Do you want masses of small blooms or fewer and larger ones? In either case it is best to remove any obviously weak shoots during the

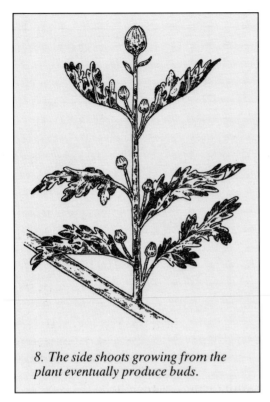

8. *The side shoots growing from the plant eventually produce buds.*

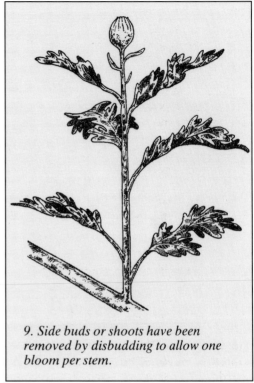

9. *Side buds or shoots have been removed by disbudding to allow one bloom per stem.*

growing time as they will not produce good results and will reduce the amount of growth in the other better shoots on the plant. However, if you want plenty of flowers for garden decoration or cutting there is no need to thin out your plants further than this.

To give you some guidance I should point out that the top exhibitor who wants best and largest blooms will often grow only two per plant whereas normal growth will produce five, six or more.

□ DISBUDDING

There are two types of cut-flower garden chrysanthemums, sprays and dis-budded blooms. You may well be growing both but there will be a difference in their treatment in mid-summer.

When the side shoots have grown sufficiently and made enough leaves they will produce buds, this time a cluster at the top of the stem (Fig. 8). (It may be of interest at this point to know that some varieties need to grow more leaves and thus longer stems than others before this required number is achieved.) This affects to some extent both plant height and flowering time. If you do nothing and allow all these buds to develop, you will have a spray. If you remove all the side buds and leave just one centre bud to develop on each shoot, you will have a bloom. This removal is called disbudding (Fig. 9).

While all chrysanthemums will produce sprays naturally, there are certain varieties which have been bred and selected for spray growth and others for blooms so that it is better to obtain the special spray varieties if you require this form of flower. They are all set out in catalogues and if you have no knowledge of any particular variety names, the nurseryman will be pleased to send you a collection suitable for your purpose.

To summarize, if you are able to provide a reasonable loam soil and you simply plant and support your chrysanthemums as they grow, with an occasional watering in dry weather, and do nothing else to them, you will get in the autumn a small bush with spray blooms on each shoot suitable for cutting or for garden decoration. If you require individual larger blooms, you also need to disbud the shoots by removing all the side growths in late summer. Any extra treatment by feeding will improve their strength and quality but is not essential for enjoyment of the flowers.

□ VARIETIES FOR GARDEN DECORATION

Having considered the tall growing spray and bloom types, let us now give some thought to the purely decorative garden kinds such as the early-flowering Suncharms. These have recently become more popular and are well worth considering. They produce a mound about 30–45 cm (12–18 in) high and up to 60 cm (2 ft) across, covered with star-like single blooms in all the chrysanthemum colours. They are truly lovely and will enhance any chosen site in the garden.

Their cultivation is not difficult. They should be planted as already suggested for garden chrysanthemums but spaced about 1 m (3.5 ft) apart to allow for growth. No stopping or supporting is needed and, of course, no disbudding. They, in fact, give maximum return for minimum attention. As with all chrysanthemums, should a hot dry spell occur soon after planting they will benefit from a good soak. In ordinary weather when the soil is moist and the humidity average, a spray overhead will help to minimize wilt due to the disturbance of the roots during planting.

It is not uncommon for both late- and early-flowering Charm chrysanthemums to make buds early in the season; this does not mean there is anything wrong with them. It is their habit of growth and they then develop shoots from soil level which grow on to provide the bush growth for the autumn. In fact some of the Suncharms will give attractive flowers in late spring and then their real display in autumn. There are few plants more attractive than garden Charms towards the end of summer and into the autumn. They provide a mass of colour, require no special attention and they give good returns.

If you really want to give minimum attention, I recommend the recently introduced hardy chrysanthemums called Spartans. They will withstand winter conditions in the open garden and keep growing from year to year. The

treatment is similar to other garden types and you can disbud them for one bloom per stem or leave them to grow naturally as sprays.

GREENHOUSE-FLOWERING VARIETIES

The cultivation of what are termed mid-season and late varieties, that is those which flower about mid-autumn until early winter, is a little more exacting but of course the bloom at that time of the year is of great value. There is a wide range of choice from spray, large single blooms, decoratives, both reflexed and incurving, to the very lovely ball-like incurved and the breathtaking Large Exhibition types; or, if you wish, you can grow Charms for house decoration, cascades of small star singles, bonsai, or windowsill plants, which can be flowered at any time of the year – a real Aladdin's cave of delights.

For the cultivation of the more usual mid- and late-flowering blooms, it is first necessary to have some sort of protection available during flowering time; ideally this would be a greenhouse or conservatory with sufficient heat to keep out the frost and particularly to prevent too high humidity. An unheated greenhouse will limit the range of possibilities, but is still worthwhile.

□ FIRST POTTING
The basic method of growing on after

'Lilian Hoek'. One of the garden flowering sprays which has remained a favourite for many years.

rooting the cuttings or receiving them from the nursery is to pot the plants into 8 cm (3 in) pots, then 13 cm (5 in) and subsequently 20 cm (8 in) using one of the three potting mixtures already mentioned.

When preparing for potting the mixture should be moist enough to hold together when squeezed in the hand. Place a layer of soil at the bottom of the 8 cm (3 in) pot of sufficient depth so that when the potting is completed, the ball of roots is comfortably covered. Place the plant on this with the roots spread and not doubled under, fill the pot up to the rim and then firm the compost down fairly hard with the thumbs and fingers so that the plant stands upright and there is sufficient space left to enable watering to be carried out. If the soil is normally moist, as mentioned earlier, it is better not to water immediately. Many plants are spoiled by overwatering just after potting: the roots have not begun to use the soil and they need air spaces to help them grow; if these are continually filled with water they, in effect, drown.

If you have potted them in the early part of the year, place them in an open position in the greenhouse with good light and ventilation and leave them for a few days. Later in the spring, when the sun begins to get warm, they may become too dry and shrivel. This can be counteracted by either a spray over as necessary for two or three days, or protection from full sun.

The other danger in late winter is a sufficiently hard frost to damage them. This should pose no problem if you have artificial heat available, but in an unheated greenhouse trouble can occur. A couple of thicknesses of newspaper over the plants for the night should be sufficient.

Do not over protect your plants; chrysanthemums like cool, airy conditions and are best left to dry out before watering again. Then fill the space at the top of the pot, giving a good soak. After a week or so the plants should have made sufficient progress so that from early spring onwards they can be put out into a frame. Again the only real danger to be aware of is frost. After a few weeks they will have made sufficient growth to necessitate potting on into 13cm (5in). Most people use plastic pots as they are lighter and cheaper than clay; these are quite suitable. Again, you can choose between the three types of potting mixture.

Extra drainage is advisable for the large pots if you are using a soil mixture. This traditionally meant broken pieces of pot placed over the hole in the bottom of the pot and covered with a layer of smaller pieces to a depth of about ¾ in. An alternative often used now is coarse gravel placed similarly at the bottom. If you are using one of the peat-based composts then this is not essential because the mixture is firmed down rather less and drainage is easier.

□ POTTING ON FOR THE SECOND STAGE

How do you know when a plant is ready to be potted on? It can be detrimental to pot on too soon so it is quite important to know. After a plant has been potted and has had time to settle into its new quarters, it is seen to grow well, increasing in height and leaf quantity and the colour of the foliage is medium to dark green. This will continue for a few weeks; just how long depends on the time of the year and the light and temperature. Obviously a warm sunny spring will bring the plants on more quickly than a cold dull one.

Among the first signs that potting on is necessary is an increasing demand for water, drying out every day or in hot weather even faster. If at the same time the foliage looks pale, hard and less fleshy, then you can be fairly certain. Obviously you cannot leave it until this check in growth has become serious and so you need to decide as soon as the first symptoms appear. All that is necessary is to knock out the plant and check the ball of soil. In the early stages after potting, little root is apparent. Gradually a network develops and finally if left alone, the roots completely cover the surface of the soil, turn into a tangled mass and a harmful check to the plant occurs. Do not pot when little root is visible nor leave it until the last stage is reached. The correct time to pot on is when the ball of soil is comfortably covered by a network of roots but there is still soil visible between them.

The actual method of potting on is straightforward. Again the potting mixture should be comfortably moist, so use the squeeze test. The plant must not be dry because if you pot such a plant on it will remain a dry core for a very long time and diminish the growth which could be obtained. To ensure it is suitably wet, water it before potting. As before, put the drainage layer into place to a depth of around 2.5 cm (1 in) (this is preferable for the 13 cm (5 in) mid-size and final pot sizes, whatever soil mixture is used) and put a bottom covering of soil of a depth which will allow the old ball of soil to be 2.5 cm (1 in) below the top of the pot. When this is covered it will leave sufficient space for watering. If you are using the traditional soil mixture you should firm down the layer at the bottom with a potting stick or rammer. This can be the wooden stem of a spade cut down to about 38 cm (15 in), one end left square and the other sharpened to a blunt wedge. Position the plant centrally upon this layer of soil, fill in with compost around the ball of soil and ram it down firmly while rotating the pot. Just cover the old rootball, ram the top a little and you have a plant suitably potted into the mid-size pot.

Finish off by making sure your name label is satisfactory and put in place a stick or cane about 45 cm (18 in) long, to which you can tie the plant. It is much better to do it at this stage, even though it may not need it, rather than leave it and find later that the plant has either fallen down and probably bent by growing upwards again, or at worst perhaps broken off.

Stand the newly potted plant on an open greenhouse bench or put it into a frame covered with lights so that it will not get too wet from rain. After a week or so the plants should go into a frame in any case, as the moist, cooler open air will grow them on better.

If you have decided to use an ordinary soil-based mixture such as is available at garden centres, less firm ramming is advisable; while a peat mixture needs no ramming at all, but just firming down with the thumbs and fingers. The mid-size 13 cm (5 in) pot will take the plant on satisfactorily until final potting is due in early summer.

The framelight covering the frame when the plants are first put in should be gradually propped up to give more air and then in late spring removed altogether, unless there is an obvious danger of night frost. Frames should be sufficient protection in themselves, but occasionally a covering of newspaper under them may be called for. It is useful to remember that frame lights made from polythene give less frost protection than glass ones.

During the later part of the spring season if the plants stay in mid-size pots they may begin to exhibit symptoms of starvation, as mentioned earlier, in relation to the 8 cm (3 in) stage. It is better to feed them once or twice than to pot them into finals too soon. Use a liquid fertilizer, classed as high nitrogen, that you will find in most garden centres and use it exactly to the maker's instructions.

□ STOPPING GREENHOUSE-FLOWERING VARIETIES

During the stay in mid-size pots the dreaded stopping and timing demon raises its head. In fact, there is truly nothing to be feared from this part of growing. As previously mentioned in relation to early garden types, the growing plant will under certain day length,

PREPARING YOUR OWN SOIL MIXTURE

For those who wish to try the old and traditional way of growing, the following is the way to produce and prepare the soil mixture.

If possible, six months or so before potting time obtain some suitable turf. This should be from an area of medium heavy soil of the marl type. Sometimes it has a reddish colour, sometimes yellowish, but it is quite different from the black peaty soils or the light sandy and lime-based ones. A good test is to cut a piece of turf about 10cm (4in) thick, containing plenty of root fibre, and drop this from a height of about 2m (6.5ft). If it keeps its cohesion and does not shatter, it has the right fibre content. Next, squeeze it in your hand and if it stays compressed it is right for texture. Its acidity should be pH 6.5.

A sufficient amount of this turf should be stacked in a corner placing the grass side downwards and, if available, a layer of farmyard manure between the layers of turves. Leave this over the winter, preferably protected from rain, and by the time you are ready for potting it will be in prime condition with the grass and roots partly rotted down, providing the necessary fibrous content.

To prepare your potting soil chop down a quantity of the heap into a soil with fibrous lumps. For first potting put it through a 2.5cm (1in) riddle and use it as it is. For mid-size and final potting make a mixture of six parts chopped loam, one part leaf mould or peat and one part old stable manure. To each 50kg (112lb) add one 8cm (3in) pot of bone meal or hoof and horn and also powdered fertilizer, according to the maker's instructions. Mix these well by turning the heap over three or four times and store in a dry place for two or three weeks before use. As a guide 22kg (50lbs) of mixture will pot about ten plants from mid- to final pots.

If you decide to use a ready-made soil-based mixture it must be prepared from a suitable type of loam. You should therefore be careful to buy it from a reliable supplier who will ensure its suitability. Poor soil can make poor compost.

temperature and maturity conditions produce buds. If left to itself a bud will form on the single stem called a break bud. This is followed by side shoots developing, which together make a plant of five or six shoots. These will in turn produce buds and at the correct time of the year will develop into flowers. Some varieties can be left entirely to their own devices and need no interference; these are said to need a natural break. Others, if left alone, would still make flowers but because of their genetic make-up they would be inferior. These are the ones which need stopping, that is, having the top of their stem pinched off (Fig. 10).

When this should be done depends on the variety, and instructions are given in chrysanthemum specialists' catalogues for each kind. An alternative is to pinch all your plants when about 20cm (8in) high and again in early summer, and then leave them to develop (Fig. 11).

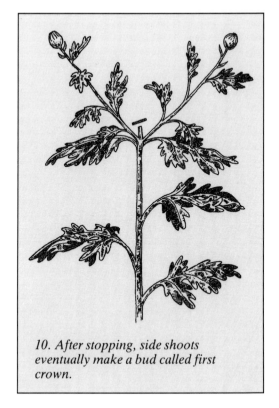

10. *After stopping, side shoots eventually make a bud called first crown.*

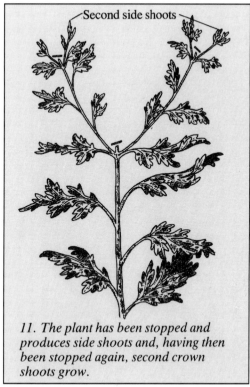

Second side shoots

11. *The plant has been stopped and produces side shoots and, having then been stopped again, second crown shoots grow.*

Some will not produce to their full potential but they will almost certainly be fine for cut flower decoration.

While early garden varieties normally flower on the first crown buds, some late-flowering greenhouse varieties are recommended as flowering on second crown. This means that the first crown buds are pinched out, causing further side shoots to grow. These in their turn make buds and develop into a flower (Fig. 12A). However, if it is indicated that a variety needs a natural second crown flower, no stopping is needed and the sequence is first the break bud, followed by side shoots which form first

crown buds (Fig. 12B). These in turn die away and are followed by side shoots which eventually make buds, called second crown (Fig. 12C).

□ POTTING ON INTO FINAL POTS

In late spring you should prepare for potting into finals. You will need compost, canes or sticks and something to tie them up with. If you are using traditional soil mixture you will have to chop down the turf from which the soil is produced, leaving lumps up to the size of a walnut. That is about twice as large as used for mid-size potting. It is

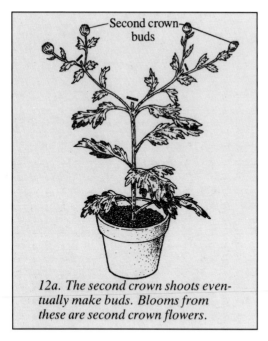

12a. *The second crown shoots eventually make buds. Blooms from these are second crown flowers.*

12b. *Plants not stopped in due course produce first crown shoots and then second crown shoots naturally.*

12c. *The second crown shoots after a natural break make buds for flowering.*

beneficial to make ready the soil a couple of weeks before potting and to have it at the correct dampness.

Clean pots of about 20 cm (8 in) size are best. Place a 2.5 cm (1 in) layer of crocks or stones into the bottom for drainage purposes; ram a layer of soil on this, using some of the turf lumps. Judge the amount by knocking the plant out of the mid-size pot and arranging it with the ball of soil about 5 cm (2 in) below the top of the pot. Fill in around the sides with soil, ramming until you have just covered the old ball of soil (Fig. 13). The freshly potted plant should be firmly potted to the point where it is quite difficult to push in the label. This kind of traditional mixture should not be too wet or too fine in texture; if it is, it will solidify in the pot, particularly if it

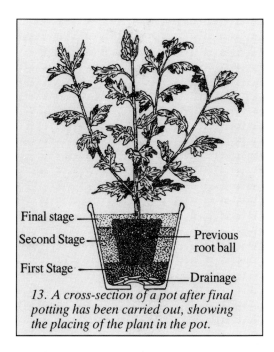

Final stage

Second Stage — Previous root ball

First Stage

Drainage

13. A cross-section of a pot after final potting has been carried out, showing the placing of the plant in the pot.

has too little fibre from its turf content.

If you are using peat- or soil-based mixture from a garden centre or nursery, ramming is not necessary but the plants should be firmly potted.

It is a good plan to secure your plants to a cane or stick after potting, the height of which should depend on the normal height of the plant. If you are unable to check this, a 1.5 m (5 ft) one will be satisfactory. Push it firmly into place and tie the plant once or more depending on its immediate needs. Do not tie too tightly as the stem will thicken as the plant grows and you must leave room for this. Sometimes when using peat mixtures the compost is not sufficiently hard in the pot for a cane to hold up easily. However, this will alter as the roots begin to grow and hold the

compost together and it should cause no trouble eventually. After potting move the plants into their summer quarters in a suitable part of the open garden.

□ SUMMER QUARTERS

The ideal situation for the summer standing ground is away from trees or shrubs but with protection from any severe winds, on a grass base where lines of slabs or similar can be laid running north to south, giving sun access to both sides of the rows. The lines of plants should be about 90 cm (3 ft) apart. Obviously ideals are rarely obtained but the nearer to this the better. It is also advisable to prepare for any wind which may be strong enough to blow over the plants. A little later in the summer when they are bigger, and more vulnerable, they may be broken off, thereby wasting a season's effort. The traditional – and probably still the best – way to do this is to knock in a strong post at each end of the row, firmly set so that about 1.5 m (5 ft) is left above ground level. Fasten a stout wire at a height of about 1.2 m (4 ft) and tie each cane firmly to this. At the same time, wind the twine around the wire as well as around the cane so that it will prevent the plant from sliding along and still being damaged, or obtain some wire clips from a sundries supplier which are specially made for the purpose (Fig. 14). All these extra jobs may sound a bit irritating but you must consider them as an insurance policy and much better done first rather than later, when numerous plants have already been broken.

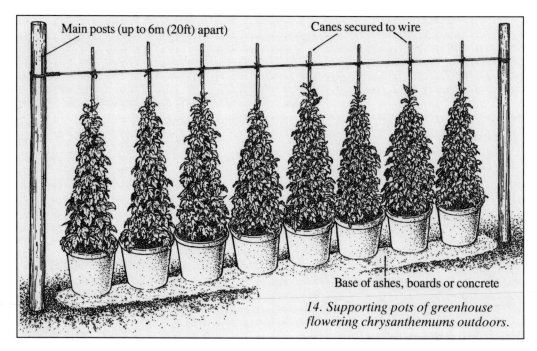

Main posts (up to 6m (20ft) apart)   Canes secured to wire

Base of ashes, boards or concrete

*14. Supporting pots of greenhouse
flowering chrysanthemums outdoors.*

WATERING POTTED PLANTS

Watering is important with pot plants at any stage and particularly so during the final pot period. At first there is a considerable amount of fresh soil not containing any roots. If overwatered this will go sour and the plant will weaken or even die due to poor root development. To add to the situation, freshly potted plants often flag for a day or two if the weather is hot, encouraging the belief that they should be watered. Do resist the temptation; for several days just spray them over once or twice a day, morning and evening if you can, and they will soon begin to establish and cease flagging. After this watering should be done by filling the space at the top of the pot as necessary. Do *not* overwater, even if the soil looks dry.

Provided the leaves are not flagging, they do not need water. When a normally developing plant which has been potted for more than a week or two flags it will be in need of water, but even then do not water it that afternoon or evening; wait until the next morning so you can be sure it needs it.

The general rule is, if you have any doubt do not water, check in the morning and see how fresh the plant looks then. Overwatering causes the plant to go yellow, leaves to flag and growth to cease, ultimately killing it. Underwatering makes foliage go dark and greyish, the plant remains flagged and the stem seems harder and thinner than usual. It would however have to be grossly underwatered to kill it. If you find you have overwatered one of your plants, carefully knock it out of its pot, give it half a turn and let it drop back in loosely. The air spaces around the side will soon encourage improvement.

□ SUMMER FEEDING

There should be no need to give any additional feed to your plants at first. The traditional soil mixtures will contain sufficient food for about a month, peat mixtures for two to three weeks. Traditional soil needs feeding about once every two or three weeks, other composts every week.

There are two basic types of fertilizer which are suitable, powdered or liquid. Either of these can be obtained and the general type needed is a tomato fertilizer with adequate potash in its make up. Liquid is easier for most people to use but powder is needed less frequently. If you are able to make it, top dressing is an excellent way to feed chrysanthemums during the latter half of the growing season. It is excellent used at intervals of about one month, from mid-summer to early autumn.

A suitable special chrysanthemum fertilizer should be mixed according to the maker's instructions with finely sieved soil, and about 1 cm (⅜ in) of this spread on top of the original soil in the pot. Not only does this provide food as it is watered in, but new feeding roots grow into it and are valuable at this later stage of the growing season.

If you do not wish to use this method, a suitable liquid feed is satisfactory (again, according to the manufacturer's instructions). For the first few times a high nitrogen feed is useful but from late summer use one which has a high potash content as this helps bud formation and development. Remember, either a special chrysanthemum fertilizer or one suitable for tomatoes will be fine.

There is no real advantage in feeding after housing the plants in early autumn, and overfeeding can in fact be harmful.

HOW MANY SHOOTS FOR EACH PLANT?

Stopping and timing may still be needed during the summer growing stage but few plants are stopped later than early summer and most by late spring. To get good quality flowers you will have to limit the number of shoots per plant. During late summer decide on your needs: plenty of flowers from many shoots or larger blooms from fewer. Decorative types give good quality at about four per plant and you can increase this to six quite reasonably if the plant is growing strongly. The true incurved ball-shaped bloom will rarely be produced at more than four per plant and may be better limited to that; while Large Exhibition varieties, the big mopheaded ones, are usually grown to produce one or at the most two blooms. Singles can safely carry six or seven shoots to flowering. If you are growing for sprays and are not disbudding the shoots then five or six per plant should be satisfactory.

In training the Large Exhibition varieties the buds are 'taken' – that is, the side growths or buds are removed – in the late summer. Most of the other types are done in early to mid-autumn. Disbudding, which means removing the side shoots whether or not they have at that stage formed buds, should be carried out when they are sufficiently developed so that they can be broken off in the leaf axil at the base of the shoot without damaging the main bud. (See under garden-flowering varieties). After disbudding, this one main bud per shoot will provide the flower.

□ PREPARING FOR FLOWERING

Although the late autumn- and winter-flowering varieties are grown outside in the open all summer, they will not withstand much frost and their blooms need protection from rain and wind. This means that they are mostly given greenhouse protection from early autumn, otherwise known as housing. If a greenhouse is not available, a framelight or polythene top cover must be provided. A conservatory can be just as effective, if you can give sufficient ventilation while the plants are inside.

PEST AND DISEASE PREVENTION

The conservatory or greenhouse must be as clean as possible from pests and disease. You will have been growing other plants and steps must be taken to clear any harmful build-up before housing your chrysanthemums. If possible, it is a good idea to wash down the greenhouse with disinfectant to help remove the danger. In any case, clean out all dead leaves and old vegetation.

When bringing in your plants give them a good drench with a fungicide such as benomyl to help control powdery mildew, which in the close conditions of a greenhouse can rapidly build

up. When doing this lay the whole plant over on its side on the ground. This will enable you to cover the top and bottom of the leaves easily.

Take the plants in and place them with the tallest in the middle and the shortest on the sides and turn on all the ventilation you have. It is also best to fumigate against insect pests by giving at least one treatment of an aphicide, and perhaps benomyl and tecnazene against the fungus diseases. This treatment before the flowers open will have long term benefits for the plants.

GREENHOUSE CONDITIONS

Your chrysanthemums will be in the greenhouse from early autumn through to winter, and so far as possible a moderate temperature and plenty of air will be beneficial. If in the first period the greenhouse becomes too hot during sunny days, a little temporary shade will help prevent petal scorch. During this time no artificial heating is necessary. It would only force growth.

As we reach the late autumn however the picture changes. Days can be warm but on still nights the humidity becomes very high. Full ventilation in day time will be necessary and, should there be any bloom damping, a little heat at night is worthwhile. It is best if a night temperature of around 13°C (55°F) can be maintained.

Should you not have heat available you must ensure that adequate ventilation is maintained day and night.

'Pennine Tango'. Recommended as an excellent garden variety for cut flower.

Nowadays a fan without a heater can be purchased quite cheaply and this, by moving the air, makes a tremendous difference at this stage and throughout the flowering period.

PESTS AND DISEASES

It is perhaps as well to consider what problems may be caused by pests and diseases and how to deal with them. The chrysanthemum is a plant which is not unduly affected but it would be wrong to pretend that there was nothing likely to harm your plants.

First, if plants are grown well and are healthy they have a natural resistance which minimizes trouble, but they may still need to be assisted. As you would expect, there are a few ubiquitous trouble-makers such as aphids, and some uncommon or rare occurrences which need mentioning but not worrying about.

□ PESTS

APHIDS
Known to most gardeners as greenfly or, as the case may be, blackfly, they will quite suddenly multiply on a plant which had appeared clear previously and will also make their home in the unfolding petals of blooms. There are in fact five different species which may affect your chrysanthemums but it is not necessary to be able to differentiate between them. In appearance they vary in size and are either green or black in colour. There are two distinct forms, winged and unwinged. The winged forms are found at the end of the winter; after fertilization they fly upwards and scatter widely, aided by warm air currents. If one of these insects lands on a chrysanthemum it will quickly give birth to live young and without further fertilization found a rapidly increasing colony. This is why they often seem to have appeared suddenly from nowhere.

Apart from recognizing the insect, look out for mottling of leaves and distortion of the growing tips due to their practice of sucking the sap. You may also see small drops of honeydew on lower leaf surfaces which become covered by a sooty mould. These conditions can clog up the pores through which the leaves breathe, and in themselves cause weak growth.

Left alone aphids can be very detrimental both because of this and because they carry virus infection by sap transference. They may be present in a greenhouse all through the year but outside only become active as the weather warms up. Do not let them build up into a significant population.

Control is a matter of persistence. It is however best to vary the chemicals used, as resistance can build up over a period. A greenhouse is easy to fumigate and smoke capsules can be obtained from any horticultural supplier. Gamma-HCH or dimethoate, malathion, pirimicarb and oxydemeton-methyl are available under proprietary names and should be used according to instructions.

Instead of fumigating, spraying can be just as effective, particularly if the attack is limited and only a shoot or two is affected. Use one of the small polythene spray bottles with graduation marks, to enable you to measure accurate volumes. It is safer to wet the underside of the leaves too. Spray is normally used in the open garden. It is best not to spray under glass or outside in strong summer sunshine in case scorching occurs. It is also advisable to spray or fumigate buds which are just opening, to eliminate aphids and prevent them from crawling into a half open bloom when they are impossible to eliminate. A flower that has been attacked eventually begins to lose its freshness and looks tired.

EARWIGS
These can cause considerable damage both to foliage in the young shoots and to blooms. Holes appear and pieces are cut out. The insect is approximately 2.5 cm (1 in) long and has a tough brown body with a pair of pincers at the back. If you see damage during the day time, give the shoot or flower a sharp shake and watch for the insect to drop out. It can then be crushed. Sometimes you have to search for it in a flower and pull it out. Gamma-HCH as a spray is effective but should only be used at about half-normal strength on flowers.

LEAF MINER
This is as common and as sudden in appearing as aphids. The first sign is often the discovery that some leaves have a network of wavy lines covering them. The lines are caused by the grub of the small fly, having hatched out from an egg laid in the chrysanthemum leaf, then rapidly eating the tissue between the top and bottom skin of the leaf leaving an ugly scar even if killed. It is therefore important to recognize it in its earliest state when many pin head sized cream spots appear just after hatching out. Attack it then and you will kill it; leave it until it has become established and the lines have formed and you will have difficulty, especially when the grub has turned into a pupa, when it is very resistant to attack. In fact if you only have a few grubs to deal with, crushing them between finger and thumb is often the easiest way of dealing with the pest. Otherwise fumigate or spray as for aphids with malathion, dimethoate, or pirimiphos-methyl, but you *must* use them in the young larval stage when the peppered spots are apparent.

SLUGS AND SNAILS
These can cause havoc in stock beds of old stools where the new cuttings are developing in spring. Sometimes if the attack is severe there seem to be no cuttings growing at all as they are eaten as fast as they grow. Fortunately there is no need nowadays to go around at night with a torch, or to set trays baited with beer! We have excellent chemicals to check them. Use a scattering of brown metaldehyde or blue methiocarb pellets; both are effective but I think I prefer the latter.

THRIPS
These are rarely seen, being very small winged insects. However, the effects are quite obvious, mostly during warm still weather in mid-summer, as their old name thunder flies suggests. Young foliage shoots display signs of distortion and mottling and petals are covered

with tiny speckles of light or dark mottling, according to the colour of the bloom. Fortunately, they cease to cause trouble in early autumn, as soon as the cooler nights arrive. To control them, a morning spray with clear water is often effective but when necessary spray with half-strength gamma-HCH or malathion, preferably morning or evening to prevent scorching.

CATERPILLARS
These can at times cause considerable trouble, particularly under greenhouse conditions. Foliage or petals are eaten and the culprit is rarely apparent. Check first for earwigs, then for slugs (the slime is usually visible) then give the stem a sharp tap and see whether or not a caterpillar drops out. Sometimes in blooms they need searching for. Pick them out and crush them if possible; otherwise spray with gamma-HCH.

CAPSID, MIRID OR 'BISHOP BUG'
This can cause some trouble during mid- and late summer. You rarely see it but its effect is found later when the developing blooms grow on one side only – the other not developing – or young growing shoots become distorted. Since it is not obvious at the time, a spray with gamma-HCH every week or 10 days during that period is usually worthwhile as a protective measure.

EELWORM
This can be a persistent pest. It is microscopic and feeds on leaf tissue. If you obtain your plants from a reliable source of supply you should not have any worry from it.

□ DISEASES
Diseases affect chrysanthemums as they do any other living subject, and again some are more troublesome and frequent than others. Fungus attacks in various forms cause harm, particularly if the plants are grown in humid conditions.

POWDERY MILDEW
This is very liable to appear during the growing season on older plants. As its name suggests, a white powdery deposit appears, first on the underside of leaves, but if left it will cover the whole plant and seriously check it. To control it, remove any old bottom leaves which may be badly affected and drench both top and underside of the leaves with benomyl. If the plants are in a greenhouse, fumigating a couple of times may be effective.

BOTRYTIS
Sometimes called grey mould, this may cause problems at the flowering stage either on garden blooms under a polythene cover or in a greenhouse. The trouble first appears as brown spots on petals and rapidly spreads into patches which can destroy the whole flower. High humidity is the main problem and it can be checked by any form of air movement or drying. Spraying or fumigating with benomyl or thiophanate-methyl will help control it.

RUST
There are two forms of this disease which can cause problems.
The old established chrysanthemum rust *Puccinia chrysanthemi* (Fig. 15) is now

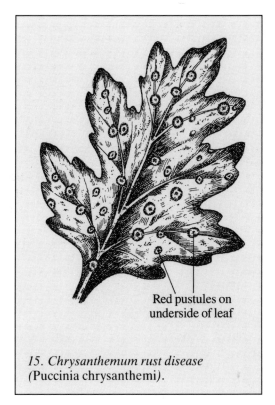

Red pustules on
underside of leaf

15. Chrysanthemum rust disease
*(*Puccinia chrysanthemi*).*

not all that common and should cause little trouble. If it appears, you will notice pale spots on the upper surface of the leaf and underneath there will be pustules of reddish brown spores, often appearing as rings. Control may be achieved by spraying, particularly on the bottom surface of the leaf with thiram.

White Rust *P. horiana*. This has become more troublesome in recent years. It was until then only occasionally found on chrysanthemum nurseries, having been imported with plants or flowers from the European mainland, Japan or the United States of America. It was viewed seriously as there was no treatment against it and if an outbreak occurred it had to be notified to the Ministry of Agriculture, with all accompanying plants having to be destroyed. It is now controlled by spraying with Tumbleblite (propiconazole) special fungicide.

In appearance it is similar to red rust but the spots are larger and the underside of the leaf shows a raised tuft of spore-bearing organs in a circular form and of fawn-white colour. Rather like a small velvety cushion.

There are other diseases which occur but they are not usually problems for the amateur grower who purchases from a reliable source. Some virus infection and wilts can be damaging but should not reach the ordinary gardener.

LOCAL RESTRICTIONS ON CHEMICAL USE

There are now quite considerable restrictions in many countries on the use of horticultural chemicals by amateur growers and you may not be able to purchase or use some of those mentioned. Please check locally.

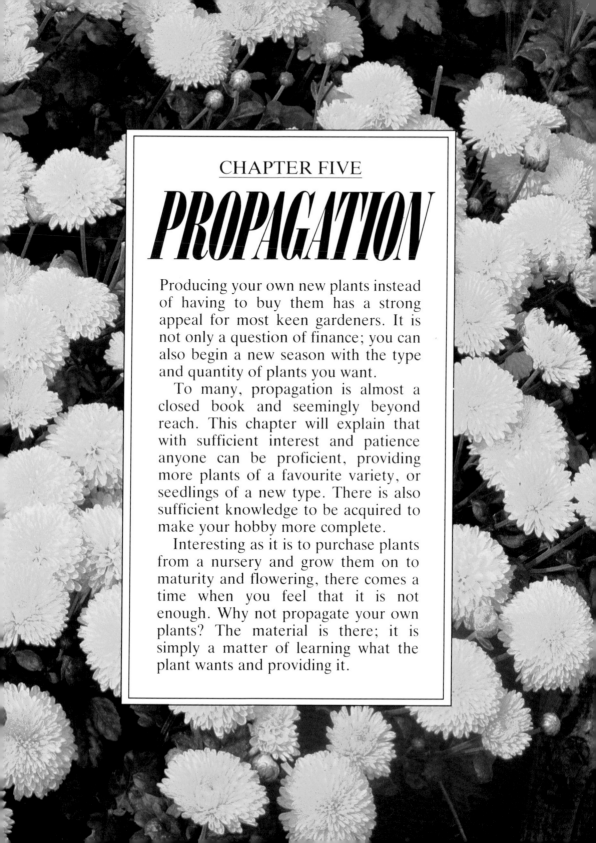

CHAPTER FIVE

PROPAGATION

Producing your own new plants instead of having to buy them has a strong appeal for most keen gardeners. It is not only a question of finance; you can also begin a new season with the type and quantity of plants you want.

To many, propagation is almost a closed book and seemingly beyond reach. This chapter will explain that with sufficient interest and patience anyone can be proficient, providing more plants of a favourite variety, or seedlings of a new type. There is also sufficient knowledge to be acquired to make your hobby more complete.

Interesting as it is to purchase plants from a nursery and grow them on to maturity and flowering, there comes a time when you feel that it is not enough. Why not propagate your own plants? The material is there; it is simply a matter of learning what the plant wants and providing it.

There are two basic ways of propagating chrysanthemums: by vegetative means, that is by rooting cuttings, and by cross pollinating and producing seeds which can be sown for the next season's growth and flower. In fact each method is used with a different purpose in view.

If you have certain varieties which you prefer and you would like to produce more plants of them yourself rather than buy them in again, you have to take cuttings. Chrysanthemums reproduce the same variety only by means of vegetative propagation. However, if you feel you would like to breed some entirely new varieties, different from those already available, you must use seed production. Every seedling is to some degree unique and it is a very interesting section of chrysanthemum growing.

Since most gardeners simply want to grow their own young plants I will first consider propagation by means of cuttings. Although the actual rooting process does not begin until the spring, autumn and winter treatment of the old plants, known as stools, is an important part of the operation. You have to produce good cuttings before you can turn them into good plants.

TREATMENT OF STOOLS

Once again we are considering the process more for the production of flowers for the garden and house decoration than for exhibition. At the same time it is better done correctly. When the plant has finished flowering it should be cut down to a height of about 30 cm (12 in) and any dead or damaged foliage removed. Do not be tempted to cut it right down to ground level, because it is too big a shock for the plant and can severely check or even kill it. Having cut it down, take care not to overwater it; while it still has leaves it needs water to replace that which is lost. Once they have gone this almost ceases and continuing to water the plant will soon harm it. Stools of the garden-flowering type should be dug up, the soil washed off, and then planted in a box of light peaty soil about 20 cm (8 in) deep. After watering them in, no more need be given for some days or even weeks depending on the weather and where they are growing. The colder the conditions the less water they need. If they are subjected to near or slight frost in the winter keep them completely dry.

Just where to overwinter stools is often a problem. Ideally they are best in a cool but frost free environment with dry moving air. They may rot if kept too wet and humid. Early garden varieties are slightly more frost resistant then the greenhouse-flowering ones which may need extra protection. Stools are quite happy in a frame or unheated greenhouse so long as protection can be given during periods of hard winter frost in the form of newspaper over the stools or some blanket type covering over the frame. Obviously light is still necessary and any covering should be removed whenever possible. Should you have no

'Anna Marie'. A lovely garden flowering spray variety which is well worth growing for decoration.

greenhouse or frame, a shed, outhouse or even a spare bedroom will suffice. Remember though, that only if they are in a heated place will they need watering.

The longer days and warmer conditions of spring will bring new growth and watering can gradually commence. Stools from a frame can be brought into the greenhouse and new basal shoots will soon appear. If they are too early for your needs cut them down to one or two leaf joints above the soil and quite soon fresh ones will develop. This can be repeated if necessary. When to begin rooting your cuttings depends on your needs and facilities. It can be any time between mid-winter and late spring but in practice late winter to early spring is probably best if you have some heat available. If not leave it until mid-spring.

ROOTING FACILITIES

Heat being available does not necessarily mean a greenhouse heated at all times but a propagating box or frame made up for the purpose. What we are aiming for are conditions of protected humidity where the cuttings will stay alive long enough for new roots to grow. When a shoot is growing from the base of a stool it uses the roots of the old plant for its water supply. Water is drawn up the stem and lost through the pores of the leaf. When a cutting is

A mixed collection of Korean spray varieties. These are more hardy than most ordinary chrysanthemums and excellent for garden flowering.

taken the supply through the roots is cut off. If this shoot is left out in ordinary dry conditions it will continue to lose water, will flag and the leaves will curl inwards. This will minimize the water loss by shutting the pores through which it is taking place. If the air is really dry even that can be insufficient and the shoot will shrivel and die. If however, it is in humid air the loss is almost nil and the shoot is able to remain alive until the new roots are formed and its water supply is renewed. It is our job to provide those warm humid conditions to enable this to take place.

A propagating frame or box can be purchased complete with thermostatic control ready to plug in and use. Always ensure that it has some means of ventilation control so that suitable humidity can be maintained; too dry and the cuttings will shrivel, too wet and they may rot. If you wish to make your own propagator you need box sides about 45 cm (18 in) deep which can be placed on a bed of sand and over which a glass or polythene cover can be drawn. A rooting temperature of about 16°C (60°F) can easily be maintained by means of electric heating cables in the sand base. Shading from direct sun will be needed and newspaper will suffice. Prepare pots or boxes which will stand in it using a peat-based propagating mixture available from garden centres. If you only wish to root a few cuttings they can be inserted round the side of a suitable pot and a polythene bag placed over it, doing away with the need for a propagator. Bottom heat will still be a useful aid however.

TAKING AND ROOTING CUTTINGS

'Hazel'. The spoon shaped petals of this garden chrysanthemum make an attractive variation.

Cut off a shoot about 8cm (3in) long, remove the two bottom leaves and trim the stem below the bottom joint. Dip this into a suitable hormone rooting powder (it is not vital if this is omitted) make a hole in the compost with a cane or stick the thickness of a pencil, insert the cutting sufficiently deep so that it will stand up, and firm it with your fingers. Water it in well with a fine rose on your can and place it in the propagator. The rest is a matter of maintaining the correct conditions. In ideal conditions it should root in about 10 days.

If you are unable to provide extra heat follow the same procedure. You may have to give a bit more ventilation whenever possible and it will take 14 to 21 days to root. During the first few days the propagator can be more or less closed up, watering usually being unnecessary. On hot days, though, a spray over may be needed if it shows signs of flagging. As soon as there is evidence that it is picking up, looking fresh and green again, more ventilation is required and an occasional watering.

'Belle'. An excellent bush type single for garden decoration.

When it has rooted and is growing away remove the container from the propagator and place it on a bench shaded from full sunlight for a few days to harden it off. Following this, the plants will benefit from full sun and air and a cool position when they will soon be ready for potting up or boxing for growing on. Work on the principle that you are not rooting the plants yourself but providing conditions which will enable them to stay alive while they form new roots. There may well be a range of cutting material from very long and thin to very short and thick. To some degree this is characteristic of the variety but it is best wherever possible to choose shoots in the middle range and also those which are fresh, green and actively growing, as they will root more quickly and make better plants.

□ PROPAGATING BY SPLITTING OFF SHOOTS

It is worthwhile to mention at this point an alternative to the usual practice I have just described. It may be that you have not the time or facilities to propagate from cuttings in the manner suggested. This however does not prevent you from producing your own young plants for growing on. Any young shoots which appear through the soil begin from that part of the old stool below the surface. If you remove the soil from around a shoot you will find that under the soil it will have roots. If you cut it off below these you will have an already rooted cutting which can be grown on in the usual way. Why go to all the trouble to cut them off and re-root them then? The exhibitors will tell you that by doing so you will get a better root system and stronger growth, but certainly for ordinary cut flower or garden needs already rooted cuttings are quite adequate.

PROPAGATION BY SEED

The other method of propagation to consider is that from seeds. As previously mentioned, you cannot duplicate an existing variety by this method, as every seedling plant is to some degree different from any other, past or present. Why then bother to produce seed and grow seedling plants? The answer is that if you cross existing varieties a small percentage will, after trial, be improvements in some way and can be put on the market as new varieties. You can also usually give it a name of your choice – quite an exciting prospect.

If you wish to cross pollinate and produce your own seed this can be done. You will be able to obtain information about the method to use either from the books on the subject or from the secretary of the National Chrysanthemum Society of Britain. You

will find it an absorbing subject.

Should you not want to go to such lengths, several of the large seed firms are offering chrysanthemum seed which you can buy. This will give you the thrill of producing a completely new variety without the work involved. All you need do is to sow it in late winter to early spring just as you would ordinary garden annuals. You need bottom heat of about 16°C (60°F) and a greenhouse or conservatory which can be kept frost free. You are now ready to begin.

□ SOWING THE SEED
Prepare a seed tray with a suitable mixture such as you can buy from general horticultural suppliers, water it with a fine rose and scatter the seeds evenly over the surface. Do not be tempted to sow too closely, as overcrowding can cause damping during germination. Make sure, too, that there is plenty of space between two different crosses in the same tray so that different types are kept apart.

After sowing the seeds cover them lightly with fine sharp sand or the mixture you are using. Put the box on the heated bed with a piece of glass or polythene on top to keep in the moisture and cover this with newspaper so that any hot sun will not harm it. After seven to ten days you will see germination. Remove the paper and gradually, over a period of three or four days the glass as well, and then put the box in a cool airy place in the greenhouse as soon as the seedlings have grown and hardened sufficiently. In about two to three weeks they will be ready for pricking out, just like ordinary bedding plants.

Use a similar mixture to that for germination, either soilless or a soil and peat type, designated 'seed and potting compost'. Grow them in open conditions and when they are about 15 cm (6 in) high with good roots, they can be moved on into 15 cm (6 in) pots if they are greenhouse varieties. Early-flowering types can be either potted, boxed or planted into a prepared bed in a frame, whichever is most convenient, and planted into their flowering quarters from late spring as soon as frost danger has gone. The greenhouse-flowering ones should be potted on and grown in the normal way, being taken in for flowering in early autumn. Both types can be stopped by pinching out the tops when about 25 cm (10 in) high. Thin out the subsequent side shoots to two or three and any being grown for blooms can be disbudded in the ordinary way. Spray varieties of course do not need disbudding.

When flowering time is reached the best plants are selected for growing again from cuttings the following season, and the remainder are destroyed. Usually two or three years of trials are needed to be sure of the merit of a variety. Remember of course, that flower assessment is not the only requirement; height, strength and healthiness, are among the many other factors which need to be considered. Obviously how many you keep for future growing, and how many years they are trialled, will depend on the purpose which you have

in mind. You may only wish to produce plenty of plants inexpensively for garden display or house decoration and then a much higher percentage can be kept and one year's selection may be sufficient. In any case it is a fascinating aspect of chrysanthemum growing and well worth attempting.

If you have a new seedling which after trial seems particularly good, you may like to contact a specialist chrysanthemum nursery to see if they will test it further with a view to marketing it. This can be a very interesting outcome for your efforts.

SPORTS

In common with many other plants the chrysanthemum occasionally produces a mutation or change called a 'sport'. This is a variation from the normal for a particular variety. The cells of the part or parts affected change and cause the difference. While this can occur in any part of the plant or bloom, the most noticeable is a change of flower colour. You may for example find that a white-flowered variety has changed to yellow and this can be of any degree from a stripe in one petal to a whole flower, or even the whole plant being affected. Cuttings taken from a whole plant sport are likely to stay the new colour. Where a whole bloom sport occurs they would probably need to be taken from the stem concerned. If only a petal or two, the chances of fixing it are rather slim.

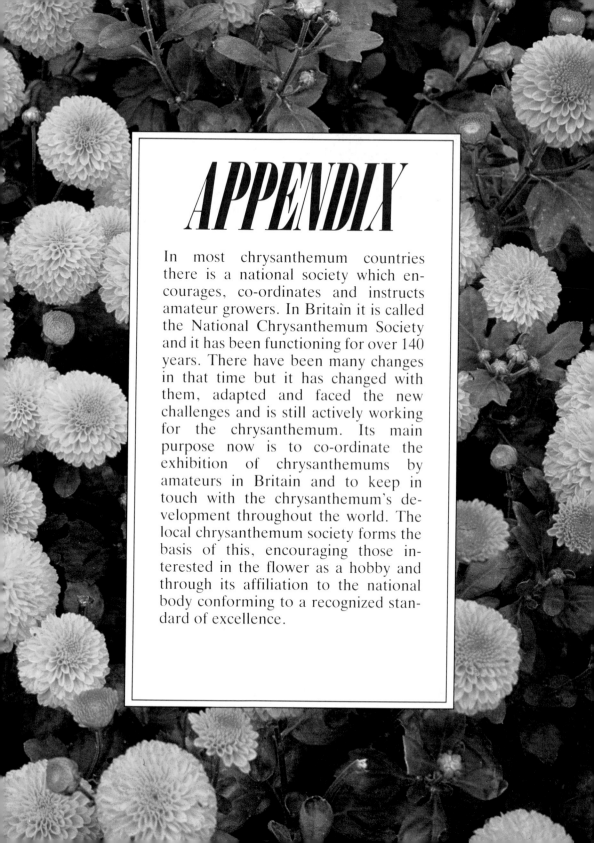

APPENDIX

In most chrysanthemum countries there is a national society which encourages, co-ordinates and instructs amateur growers. In Britain it is called the National Chrysanthemum Society and it has been functioning for over 140 years. There have been many changes in that time but it has changed with them, adapted and faced the new challenges and is still actively working for the chrysanthemum. Its main purpose now is to co-ordinate the exhibition of chrysanthemums by amateurs in Britain and to keep in touch with the chrysanthemum's development throughout the world. The local chrysanthemum society forms the basis of this, encouraging those interested in the flower as a hobby and through its affiliation to the national body conforming to a recognized standard of excellence.

Founded in 1846 in Stoke Newington, the Borough of Hackney (London) Chrysanthemum Society, as it was then called, was initially interested in fruit only, adding the chrysanthemum part of it afterwards. As was common at the time, the Society first met in a public house called the Amherst Arms in Shacklewell Lane. Instructional papers were read and an election of the best varieties was held. A report of the show held in 1852 said 'We do not exaggerate when we say that many of the blooms were six inches in diameter. A sumptuous dinner was provided and the 60 to 70 exhibitors and friends sat down to it; though beyond eating and drinking there was nothing very remarkable said or done'.

In 1877 the first real show was held at the Westminster Aquarium. 'All money taken at the door was divided into prizes and handed to the winners after they had dined'.

In 1884 the name was changed to the National Chrysanthemum Society and meetings were from that time held at the Old Four Swans, Bishopsgate Street, London. By 1890 there were 74 affiliated societies. In 1895 the first Year Book was published and this is still an annual publication.

The turn of the century was a period of great country estates, with their many gardeners taking advantage of the ample growing facilities for large numbers of plants. This was reflected by classes

'Damping' of petals caused by botrytis. This fungus attacks in conditions of humid, stagnant air.

which called for no less than 48 different varieties to be staged. Exhibitors had to transport hundreds of blooms many miles without motor transport.

In 1920 Mr. E.F. Hawes became the Society's Chairman, an office which he filled for a record 52 years. 1920 was also the year in which its first show was held in the Royal Horticultural Society's Hall at Westminster, the venue still being used for its two annual exhibitions. Publications increased and became a vital part of membership benefits, and in 1938 arrangements were made with the Royal Horticultural Society to form a joint Early-flowering Chrysanthemum Committee and to hold trials at the RHS garden at Wisley in Surrey. This was later extended to other parts of the country.

In 1950 the Northern Group of the Society was formed and this was followed by Scottish, Welsh, Midland and Southern and South Western Groups all working with the parent society. In 1951 the Society staged an exhibition at the International Show at Angers, France, and in competition with several other European countries won the Premier Prix d'Honneur offered by the President of France.

At present the Society is strong and healthy, with around 4000 members and 200 affiliated societies throughout Britain and overseas too. Close cooperation with the national societies of USA, Canada, Australia, New Zealand, India and Japan is maintained, together with frequent contact with chrysanthemum bodies in other countries.

These international contacts are of

considerable interest and value. Many overseas countries have a similar structure of local and national societies and there is an International Chrysanthemum Council. Each country has a basically similar classification system, modified to its own needs, so there is an exchange of information which helps to standardize a worldwide approach, particularly valuable when naming new introductions. Unless there is co-ordination, different varieties could carry the same name or different names could be given to the same variety. This can cause problems when plants are exchanged or bought from overseas.

Every two or three years an international meeting is arranged in one of the member countries, attended by the official national delegates and other interested growers. All take part in a programme of chrysanthemum and tourist interest. In recent years I have been to meetings in London, New York and Tokyo and have derived much pleasure from meeting other enthusiasts, hearing about their cultivation problems and realizing how widespread the hobby is. The next meeting is arranged for Perth, Australia, in 1990. Any enthusiast can join in the National Chrysanthemum Society's arrangements. Interest in chrysanthemums is truly international.

We in the United Kingdom are used to a very temperate climate and treat our plants accordingly. A day or two over 27°C (80°F) and we get worried. But meet growers from the southern United States of America or Australia and you find they regularly have to cope with summer temperatures of 38°C (100°F) or more for weeks with little or no rain. They adapt their methods and still produce excellent flowers.

It may seem surprising that there is sufficient work for a national society. Why should it be necessary when quite a small number of keen gardeners are interested in growing a few chrysanthemums? Basically because when a non-specialist gardener decides to concentrate on chrysanthemums, he is interested in joining a local society to contact others with a similar interest and this demands a formal structure with guidelines or rules.

As one's knowledge increases so does the realization that growing chrysanthemums can be a true craft. You then wish to exhibit your plants in competition with fellow members.

When organizing a show of members' flowers a local chrysanthemum society has to make rules for exhibition. If each society set out basically different conditions for entries, a keen exhibitor could hardly show anywhere but his own society's shows because blooms exhibited in the autumn have to be planned for the previous late winter or early spring – the varieties to be grown and the growing methods. So it is essential for exhibition rules to be standardized as widely as possible by the country's national body.

One of the key tasks of the national society is to define the type of bloom which best exemplifies each section, agreeing the qualities of each different type of flower. For example, incurved blooms should be as near ball shaped as possible, singles have neatly laid flat petals lying around the daisy eye. Classes are arranged for all the different types at local and national shows throughout Britain.

The two National Shows held at the RHS Halls in Westminster, one for early garden-flowering varieties in September and one for greenhouse plants in November, are the Mecca of all chrysanthemum enthusiasts, followed closely by similar exhibitions organized by the various affiliated groups. The Society's Floral Committee does considerable work in classifying and registering the new varieties which are introduced each year by specialist chrysanthemum nurserymen and takes part in the Joint RHS, NCS Chrysanthemum Committee which gives awards of excellence to them.

I can recommend any amateur chrysanthemum grower to join the Society. The annual subscription is small and in fact produces a return in excess of the payment. The member receives an annual Year Book and regular bulletins reporting on its workings and the chrysanthemum scene in general, plus many articles on general cultivation of both early- and late-flowering types, reports on new introductions, details of local affiliated societies and their shows – in fact news of every facet of the chrysanthemum world. There is an advisory service which helps to solve current problems, and passes are issued for the shows and trial grounds, currently at Wisley and Bradford. The Society offers a range of books on every aspect of chrysanthemum growing, organizes and trains judges for its registered list and offers many items of interest – among them medals and certificates – to affiliated societies.

All this, plus of course the fellowship of those with similar interests, makes it ideal for the keen grower, whether an exhibitor or ordinary gardener. Write to the Secretary, 2 Lucas House, Craven Road, Rugby, Warwickshire CV21 3JQ, England, for details.

INDEX

All the year round industry,
17–18
American origins, 17
Anemone-centred types,
54–57
  outdoor, 72
Annual beds, 34
Aphids, 102–3
Australian origins, 17

Bishop bug, 104
Bonsai types, 25–26, 68
Botrytis, 104
Bush types, 77

Capsid bug, 104
Cascade types, 24–25, 65–66
Caterpillars, 104
Charm types, 65–66, 70–71
Chinese origins, 15
Christmas-flowering, 26–27
Chrysanthemum
  'Alison Kirk', 71
  'Amethyst', 47
  'Anna Marie', 75
  'Baby', 58
  'Balcombe Perfection', 19
  'Bambi', 72
  'Belle', 75
  'Brideshead', 69
  'Bridget', 54
  'Bronze Fairie', 74
  'Bronze Fairweather', 49
  'Bullfinch', 65
  'Cameo', 18, 74
  'Carol Moonlight', 75
  'Chaffinch', 70
  'Charisma', 65
  'Charm Ringdove', 27
  'Choirboy', 57
  'Christmas Wine', 50
  'Cloth of Gold', 72

'Cloudbank', 54
'Corngold', 53
'Cossack', 47
'Denise', 74
'Doris', 75–76
'Dorridge Dream', 71
'Dorridge Velvet', 50
'Dresden', 58
'Duke of Kent', 44
'Early Red Cloak', 72
'Epic', 54
'Ermine', 18–19
'Ethel', 58
'Evelyn Bush', 19, 72
'Fairie', 74
'Fairweather', 49
'Flo Cooper', 72
'Gambit', 72
'Gigantic', 44
'Ginger', 77
'Glorietta', 50
'Gold Mine', 77
'Goldcrest', 70
'Golden Climax', 58
'Goldplate', 70
'Grace Riley', 72
'Green Goddess', 19, 47
'Green Nightingale', 27, 62
'Greensleeves', 27, 53
'Hazel', 76
'Hazel McIntosh', 53
'Hedgerow', 27, 57
indicum, 19
'James Bryant', 47
'Jessie Habgood', 19, 44
'Joan', 76
'John Hughes', 49
'John Riley', 70
'John Statham', 71
'John Woolman', 19
'Karen Riley', 70
'Kingfisher', 65

'Lakelanders', 49
'Lillian Hoek', 75
'Lindy', 47
'Lovely Charmer', 57
'Majestic', 47
'Marie Taylor', 75
'Marlene Jones', 72
'Mary Poppins', 27, 65
'May Shoesmith', 19
'Megan Woolman', 49
'Moonlight', 76
'Morning Star', 65
'Muriel Foster', 75
'My Love', 57, 68
'Ogmore Vale', 65
'Old Purple', 15
'Oyster Fairweather', 49
'Party Frock', 27
'Pennine Gambol', 72
'Pennine Jade', 75
'Pennine Oriel', 72
'Pennine Salute', 38
'Pennine Tango', 75
'Peter Rowe', 71
'Phil Houghton', 19, 44
'Pink Duke', 44
'Pink Gin', 58
'Princess Anne', 68
'Quill Elegance', 62
'Raymond Mounsey', 54
'Rayonnante', 62
'Red Admiral', 54
'Red Pixie', 65
'Red Woolman's Glory', 38
'Redwing', 70–71
'Remarkable', 77
'Riley's Dynasty', 70
'Ringdove', 65
'Robeam', 58
'Roblaze', 60
'Romark', 60
'Ryflash', 60

'Rynoon', 60
'Sally Ball', 72
'Salmon Fairie', 74
'Seychelle', 47
'Sheila Morgan', 53–54
'Shirley McMinn', 70
'Shirley Model', 19
'Shirley Primrose', 44
'Shirley Sunburst', 49
'Shoesmith Salmon', 50
sinense, 29
'Skaters Walz', 54
'Skylark', 71
'Snowshine', 54
'Spartan', 76-77
'Sunblaze', 72
'Sylvia Riley', 18
'Tang', 65
'Thumbelina', 65
'Tom Stillwell', 50
'Vera Woolman', 19
'Violet Lawson', 54
'Wagtail', 71
'West Bromwich', 50
'Woolman's Glory', 57
'Yellow Shirley Imp', 49
Church decoration, 35
Chusan daisy, 15
Classifications, 37–41
Composts for greenhouse
    types, 91–92
    for growing on, 81
Container growing, 22–24,
    28–29
Cross pollination, 114
Cut flowers, 27
Cuttings, 111–113
    bonsai, 68
    cascades, 66
    large exhibition types, 43–44
    mini-mums, 62–65
    spray types, 58

Decoratives, intermediate,
    50–54
    reflexed, 50
Disbudding, greenhouse,
    99–100
    outdoor, 88–89

Disease, 102–5
    prevention, 100

Earwigs, 103
Eelworm, 104
Exhibition types, 121
    incurved, 47–49
    large, 41–44
    medium, 44–47

Fantasies, 62
Feeding, pot-grown types, 93
    summer, 99
Ferns, 27–28
Floral art, 35
Fortune, Robert, 15
French origins, 15
Fumigation, 102

Greenhouse
    conditions, 100
    fumigation, 102
    varieties, 38–40, 41–70,
        91–100
Growing on, 81–82

Hardy types, 32, 76–77
Herbaceous borders, 30–32
Houseplants, 24
Housing, 100
Humus, 82

Incurved types, 15, 47–49,
    69–71
Indoor types, 38–68, 91–100
Insecticides, 102–3
Intermediate types, 70–72

Japanese origins, 144–15
    types, 41
Johnson, J. & T., 18

Korean types, 75–76

Lawn beds, 34–35
Leaf miner, 103

Mini-mums, 62
Mirid bug, 104

National Chrysanthemum
    Society, 15, 38, 117–21

October-flowering types, 40,
    69–70
Offshoots, splitting, 113–14
Outdoor types, 40–41, 68–69,
    81–89

Patio growing, 288–29
Pests, 102–4
    prevention, 100
Photoperiodism, 18
Planting schemes, 28–35
    time, 82–85
Pompon types, 15, 32, 57–58,
    74
Potting, first-stage, 91–92
    second-stage, 92–93
Potting-on, 95–97
Powdery mildew, 104
Propagation, 107–15
Puccinia, 104–5

Quill types, 58, 62

Reflexed types, 15
    decorative, 50
    garden, 71–72
    October-flowering, 70
Riley's, 18
Rockery types, 32–34
Rooting, 52, 111
Rowe, Frank, 19
Rubellum types, 75–76
Rust, 104–5

Seed propagation, 114–15
Shoesmith, H., 19
Single types, 57
Siting plants, 28
Slugs, 103
Snails, 103
Soil mixture, 94
    preparation, 82
    requirements, 81–82
Spartan types, 32, 34, 76–77
Specimen plants, 66–68
Spider types, 58, 62
Spoon types, 58, 62

Sports, 115
Spray types, 58–60, 74–75
Stools, 108–11
Stopping, 41–43
   greenhouse, 93–95, 99–100
   outdoor, 85–87
Summer care, 97–99

Suncharm types, 24, 29, 34,
   70–71
Supports, 97

Temperature for growing on,
   81
Thinning out, 87–88

Thrips, 103–4
Timing, 85–87

Water features, 32
Watering, greenhouse, 97–98
   outdoor, 81–84
Woolman, John, 18, 19

ACKNOWLEDGEMENTS

The publishers gratefully acknowledge the following
agencies and photographers for granting permission to
reproduce the following colour photographs: Photos
Horticultural Picture Library (pp. 12/13, 36/37, 39, 45,
48, 73, 78/79, 90 and 106/107); Jack Woolman (pp. 16,
20/21, 26, 30, 31, 65, 83 and 118); Pat Brindley (pp. 42,
64, 67, 101 and 110); the Harry Smith Horticultural
Photographic Collection (pp. 43, 46, 51, 52, 53, 56, 60,
61, 63, 69, 109, 112, 113 and 116/117). The photographs
on pp. 23, 33 and 59 were taken by Bob Challinor.
All line drawings are by Nils Solberg.